D0210053

# The Quiet Rebels

## The Story of the Quakers in America

### Margaret Hope Bacon

with an introduction
**"The Quaker Contribution to Nonviolent Action"**

## new society publishers

Inquiries regarding request to republish all or part of *The Quiet Rebels* should be addressed to:
New Society Publishers
4722 Baltimore Avenue
Philadelphia, PA 19143
ISBN: 0-86571-057-0 Paperback
0-86571-058-9 Hardcover
Printed in the United States

Cover Design by Dion Lerman

New Society Publishers is a project of the New Society Educational Foundation and a collective of Movement for a New Society. New Society Educational Foundation is a non-profit, tax-exempt public foundation. Movement for a New Society is a network of small groups and individuals working for fundamental social change through non-violent action. To learn more about MNS, write: Movement for a New Society, 4722 Baltimore Avenue, Philadelphia, PA 19143. Opinions expressed in this book do not necessarily represent positions of either the New Society Educational Foundation or Movement for a New Society.

# Contents

# Illustrations

*In Memory*
Francis Rogers Bacon

# Introduction:
# The Quaker Contribution
# To Nonviolent Action

During the Vietnam War, the sight of a group of Quakers standing in vigil before the White House or being arrested for holding a silent meeting on the steps of the Capitol was a familiar part of the nightly news. Sometimes the Quaker protesters were seen holding candles, or reading out the names of the dead; sometimes they had joined other groups in mammoth demonstrations. Their decision to send medical supplies to North Vietnam was an act of civil disobedience which created headlines throughout the United States, and won them the admiration of doves and the anger of hawks. No one questioned that their nonviolent actions were a powerful force in the growing national resistance to the unpopular war.

Yet in 1960, when the Quakers proposed to celebrate the 300th anniversary of the Quaker peace testimony with a silent vigil before the Pentagon, some conservative Friends questioned whether such public witness was the correct posture for the Society. Did it imply an element of coercion, rather than pure Christian persuasion? Did such an action appear to be motivated by the desire for publicity?

To air some of these concerns, a session was organized at Pendle Hill, a Quaker study center near Philadelphia, to explore "The Role and Responsibility of Peace Churches for Public Witness." Henry J. Cadbury, Quakerism's leading historian, spoke of the long Quaker tradition of conscientious refusal to obey the state when its demands conflicted with those of God. A whole new terminology was coming into use, he said: public witness, civil disobedience, nonviolent resistance, passive resistance, satyagraha. Mostly they were new names, he thought, for older and forgotten experience.

Members of the Religious Society of Friends use a concept which they call "Proceeding as the way opens". If you take a first step in obedience to religious impulse, a step in the Light, more Light will come. The first generation of Friends had no inkling that they might be among the pioneers of the developing movement of nonviolence when they refused to obey laws which violated their conscience. But refuse they did, until the jails of England, and to a lesser extent those of the new colonies in America, were full of them.

Their chief goal was to worship as they believed they ought. They refused to go to the established church, and to pay tithes to support the clergy. When forbidden to hold meetings, they went calmly ahead and held them anyway, although they knew they would be hauled off to prison.

Their commitment to God made it impossible for them to swear oaths, or to remove their hats to people in authority, or to have their marriages celebrated by the clergy. For these infractions too, they were punished. And although the Friends had not developed a consistent peace testimony at the very beginning of their movement, more and more individual Friends felt they could not be followers of Christ and soldiers in the army. On several occasions this insight struck so suddenly that a soldier or sailor paused in battle. Naturally, they were imprisoned for refusing to bear arms. Altogether, many thousands of men, women, and even children were thrown into jail, and many hundreds died. In the Massachusetts Bay colony, where Quakers were automatically imprisoned on arrival, four were hanged for their insistence on returning to Boston time after time to witness to their right to worship as they chose.

People at first thought the Quakers were mad, or dangerous, or both, but in time their patient acceptance of suffering and their refusal to violate their deepest beliefs had a powerful effect on public opinion and became a factor leading to religious toleration in Great Britain and religious liberty in the United States.

Friends' choice of suffering was deliberate. Edward Burroughs, one of the early travelling ministers, stated in 1661, ". . . . if anything be commanded of us by the present authority which is not according to equity, justice, and a good conscience toward God. . . . we must in such cases obey God only and deny active obedience for conscience's sake, and patiently suffer what is inflicted upon us for our disobedience to men."

They also made it a point to be open and truthful about their disobedience. When the Conventicle Act of 1661 was passed, making it illegal for more than five people to gather at a time (in an effort to do away with dissenting and radical groups), some sects met in secret and brought food along, so they might pretend to be having a meal instead of a religious service if discovered. But the Quakers met openly. When their meeting houses were occupied, they met in the public street. After those who so met were hauled off to jail, others came to take their places, with the patient insistence which was later to characterize the followers of Gandhi's satyagraha as they faced clubbing by the police and army following the Salt March. In one famous case, when both the jails of Bristol were full of

Quakers, their children continued to hold meetings, until they too were imprisoned, beaten, or placed in stocks.

Friends coupled their acceptance of suffering with a clear set of demands, another common feature of nonviolence. They wanted liberty of conscience for themselves and for other dissenters, and they petitioned the king and the parliament regularly, patiently, and persistently. They also asked that the Friends in prison be released, and at times offered their own bodies to take the place of others.

Continued persecution was an important factor in the decision of many Quakers to come to the New World. Although here too they met punishment and banishment in several of the colonies, in others there was a measure of tolerance and more space in which to set up their own settlements. Rhode Island and Long Island, New York in particular became early havens for the Friends.

But the New World brought them face to face with a new problem: the relations between the European settlers and the native Americans who were already living on the lands claimed by the colonists. At first the Indians greeted the new arrivals cordially, but the white men's assertion of ownership of their ancient lands created bitterness, and in some cases open conflict. The fact that many of the Christian settlers regarded the unbaptized Indians as "limbs of Satan," devoid of any good intention, made all peace negotiations virtually impossible.

The Quaker attitude toward the Indians was markedly different. They believed that there was "that of God," or a capacity for good in everyone, and that if they would act in accordance with their religious principles there would be a response or "answer" in the Indians. Quakers were careful to pay the Indians for their land, as opposed to simply taking it away from them on the basis of a grant or purchase made in England. They avoided giving them alcohol, knowing its injurious effects, and they addressed them as "brothers."

They even refused to join other settlers in running to the stockades at times of Indian unrest.

Some amazing incidents resulted from this policy. Quaker ministers travelling in the wilderness not infrequently came across Quaker families living unarmed and unharmed in the midst of what was regarded as hostile territory. Friends were occasionally protected and aided by Indians on their trips through the forests. Conversely, those Friends who picked up guns or went into the stockades were apt to be attacked.

The matter was discussed in the Quaker meetings, where Friends were urged to be true to the peace testimony. In one famous case, an older woman, with her grown daughter, son-in-law, and grandchildren were living in an isolated area without protection. The older woman became nervous, and persuaded her children to go with her to the stockade. On a trip out of the fort, the older woman was ambushed and killed. The younger couple decided that this murder had occurred because they had disobeyed the peace testimony, and they returned with their children to their home, "where the Indians were at our doors and windows." Here they lived without incident, leaving the children at home alone when they travelled to meeting.

Living in colonies where they were not in the majority, Quakers had to separate themselves from their European neighbors in order to make their peace with the Indians. But in the colonies of New Jersey and Pennsylvania, settled largely by Quakers, it was possible to develop a policy of friendship with the native peoples. Pennsylvania, William Penn's "Holy Experiment", was known throughout the world for its capacity to make and keep peace with the Indians. Penn went to great pains to let the native Americans know of his coming and of his desire to share the land with them, and was scrupulous about the purchase of that land. His famous treaty of Shackamaxon, made on the shores of the Delaware, lasted for seventy years.

Some historians have suggested that the Delaware Indians with whom Penn and his settlers dealt were peaceable people, and there may have been more incidents of violence between the Indians and the new settlers than have been reported in the history books. Nevertheless, the fact that the Indians and Quakers were able to coexist for so many years without warfare was regarded at the time by many Europeans as a kind of miracle, and was much discussed among those who were interested in the progress of peace.

The Quaker practice of nonviolence, as we would call it today, in support of freedom of conscience, and in keeping peace with the Indians, was coupled with its employment in Friends' struggle for the abolition of slavery. The aim was to influence state governments, and the newly formed Congress, through the medium of public opinion. In this they were unsuccessful. But a few daring Friends did help to protect the freedom of individual Blacks who had run away from their masters, or had struck out for liberty when brought to stay in the North.

Isaac Hopper, a Philadelphia tailor, often interposed his own body between the slave and the would-be slave catcher, and became known for his complete fearlessness. Lucretia Mott once followed a tar-and-feather mob which had seized an elderly abolitionist, pleading with them to take her rather than him to ride on the rail, and so thoroughly shamed the men that they let their victim go. A number of Friends went to prison rather than obey the Fugitive Slave Law or pay a fine.

The concept of using nonviolence as a weapon in an ongoing struggle, rather than as passive resistance to injustice, was born with the movement for the abolition of slavery, and found expression among the followers of William Lloyd Garrison, editor of the *Liberator* and the leader of the radical abolitionists. In 1838, Garrison and Adin Ballou, a Unitarian minister, organized the New England Non-

Resistance Society, the first group to articulate what we call a non-violent philosophy of social change.

The Non-Resisters were long on rhetoric and short on practical examples. For the latter they turned to Quaker experience with the Indians and with the Underground Railroad, a series of safe houses for runaway slaves fleeing northward to freedom, still in its early stages. Later, the non-resister abolitionists learned to use the concept of nonviolence to protect escaping slaves from slave catchers. They also began to work for the racial integration of trains, trolleys, and streetcars, and to "sit in" at churches which had not declared themselves against slavery. Philadelphia had a successful streetcar boycott, conducted by Black and Quaker abolitionists, almost one hundred years before the Montgomery bus boycott.

One aspect of the Non-Resistance movement was its alliance with a host of other radical causes, including the establishment of ideal communities, a toleration for the concept of Free Love, and Christian anarchism. Non-Resisters believed that the government in the antebellum United States supported slavery "by the bayonet," and that they themselves should not vote or hold office or serve on a jury, or otherwise be complicit in such a state.

This latter concept of the Non-Resisters was distasteful to many Quakers. While they often themselves resisted government, they believed that they ought to obey and support it whenever they were not conscientiously forced to do otherwise. Penn had believed that government could be good if run by good men. Years of persecution had probably had the effect of influencing Friends to avoid taking anti-authoritarian stands unless forced to by conscience.

The result was that though the Non-Resisters leaned heavily on Quaker practice, only a few of the more radical Quakers joined the movement, and the practice of non-resistance was decried in the pages of Quaker periodicals. Probably a larger number of

Friends shared the viewpoint that government was evil, but hesitated to go out on a limb.

One of the most prominent members of the New England Non-Resistance Society was Lucretia Mott, known also as an abolitionist and an advocate of the rights of women. She was one of a small band of Quaker abolitionists-feminists who provided most of the leadership, and at least thirty percent of the womanpower, of the women's rights movement right up to the Civil War. As a result of this interlocking of issues, the women's rights movement itself used the weapons of nonviolence in its ongoing struggles. When their meetings were met with mob violence, the women frequently refused police protection, but attempted to meet the threat with calm fortitude, closing ranks and walking two-by-two through the angry crowd.

Arrested in Ohio for distributing anti-slavery literature on Sunday, Abby Kelley Foster, a fiery Quaker from Worcester, Massachusetts, went limp and refused to cooperate in any way with her own arrest, imprisonment, or trial. Later, together with several other women, she refused to pay taxes on her farm, proclaiming "no taxes without representation." Susan B. Anthony, also a Quaker, voted illegally to protest her lack of enfranchisement, and prepared to accept a fine or imprisonment. The judge, however, refused to execute the sentence. At the time of the Centennial of the founding of the United States, Anthony and four other women interrupted the celebration ceremonies with a nonviolent protest in order to declare a women's bill of rights.

This coupling of women's rights with nonviolence continued into the twentieth century, when Alice Paul, a Quaker from Moorestown, New Jersey, led a suffrage protest which began as a peaceful vigil before the White House and ended by filling the jails of the District of Columbia with women on hunger strikes. As women were taken to jail from the picket lines, more women took their place. The protest became widely known, and played a key role in winning the Nineteenth Amendment.

Although the Non-Resistance movement died long before these events, it served its purpose in articulating the philosophy of opposing evil with active goodwill, and it collected many Quaker experiences to prove the efficacy of the method. The movement's ideas were spread widely through a newspaper, *The Practical Christian*, published by Adin Ballou from the Hopedale Community, and through Ballou's correspondence with Count Leo Tolstoy in Russia, and others. Tolstoy also corresponded with Garrison, and later with Mohandas Gandhi when the latter was a young lawyer in Durban, South Africa, first beginning to formulate his ideas about the application of Soul Force.

When Gandhi, in turn, began his nonviolent campaigns for the freedom of the Indian people, fighting for justice with the power of love and truth, many Quakers saw in his movement a positive expression of their pacifism. A few British Friends actually joined the movement, and others met with Gandhi when he visited England. After Gandhi's death, Friends kept in close touch with the Gandhian movement, and when Martin Luther King, Jr. decided to visit the sites of Gandhi's struggles, the American Friends Service Committee helped to raise the money for the trip and arranged his itinerary.

Meanwhile, Friends had been developing their own experience in the use of non-resistance. The imposition of the draft during the Civil War presented the Quaker pacifist with a dilemma; he could either pay a bounty to be excused and send another man in his place, or go into the army and refuse to cooperate. Some chose the latter course, and not a few were severely punished and even tortured in an effort to persuade them to carry guns. During the First World War, the universal draft again made no provision for conscientious objectors, and several hundred Quakers ended up in prison or in army stockades because of their refusal to cooperate. Once more, the patient acceptance of suffering had a long-term effect: in World War II there was a provision for conscientious objectors from the major peace churches, and during the Vietnam War such provisions were further broadened and liberalized.

Many of the conscientious objectors of World War I went overseas with the newly formed American Friends Service Committee to try to heal the wounds of war and demonstrate "a service of love in wartime," an alternative method of solving problems nonviolently. The unarmed volunteers found they could work on either side of the battle lines in disputed territory, so long as they carried the AFSC star and made it clear that their mission was peace. This same experience continued into the time of the Vietnam War, when the Quaker Center in Quang Ngai was never disturbed, although it was the site of some of the fighting, because it carried a sign on its door in Vietnamese and English stating:

NO WEAPONS PLEASE

Ninety percent of the patients in this Center
have suffered injuries caused by weapons.
Please leave yours outside.

A second and unexpected source of knowledge concerning the efficacy of nonviolence emerged during the Second World War, when many conscientious objectors were placed in mental hospitals on the so-called violent wards, and learned that if they would approach the most disturbed patients with trust and respect, the necessity for straitjackets and restraints of any kind disappeared.

During the past two decades, the Quakers have joined in struggles for civil rights, for an end to the Vietnam War, for human rights in Central America, and for nuclear disarmament. In this last struggle they have worked closely with the peace movement in Europe. Quaker authors have also produced a number of books on the theory and practice of nonviolence and the use of nonviolent civilian defense as an alternative to military combat.

An outgrowth of A Quaker Action Group, formed during the Vietnam War to deliver medical supplies to North Vietnam, is the Movement for a New Society (MNS), a group committed to seeking structural change through nonviolence. MNS members live simply in communities scattered throughout the United States, but the largest and most stable center has been the Life Center in Philadelphia. Life Center members believe that personal and social change go hand-in-hand, and have simplified their lifestyles in order to avoid complicity with a state and economy based on war (in a manner that reminds one of the Non-Resisters at Hopedale Community). They work in their neighborhoods as well as mounting nonviolent campaigns on international issues, and they hold regular nonviolent training sessions. Although born of Quaker leadership, MNS appeals to persons of many religious faiths.

The twentieth century has seen the development of nonviolent leadership in Africa, in Europe, and in Latin America, exemplified by such individuals as Danilo Dolci, Dom Helder Camara, Kenneth Kaunda, Chief Albert Luthuli, and Adolfo Perez Esquivel, as well as Cesar Chavez and Martin Luther King, Jr. and others in this country. Many additional groups in the United States, including the Fellowship of Reconciliation, the War Resisters League, and the Women's International League for Peace and Freedom, are advocates of nonviolence today.

Quakers have welcomed these developments, done what they could to nourish the new movements, and nominated many of the leaders for the Nobel Peace Prize. They feel that they have much to learn from the new movements, while their own long history of involvement in peace and social change activism enables them to speak with some authority on behalf of the newer groups in the United States.

Friends believe that we are today at the very beginning of discovering the potential power of nonviolence. If men and women would refuse to cooperate with unjust governments on a broad scale, such governments could not long endure. The habit of implicit obedience to authority, even when that authority becomes evil, as in the case of Hitler, needs to be broken if the people of the world are to achieve peace and justice.

At the time of World War II, the U.S. government ordered that all persons of Japanese-American descent be removed from the West Coast and placed in concentration camps. The vast majority of these persons were American citizens of unquestioned loyalty; the order was made strictly on the basis of race. Many constitutional lawyers now agree that it was one of the worst decisions ever made and upheld by U.S. courts. But the Japanese-Americans believed that they had no option but to obey. They packed their bags and left their homes in fear and sorrow.

One man, however, refused to go. Gordon Hirabayashi was a Quaker and a conscientious objector to war. He knew the order was unjust, and though he was very young at the time, he had the courage to refuse to cooperate with injustice. Instead, he went to prison. What would have happened, we can ask, if thousands of other Japanese-Americans had refused to go? Or if the whole town of Dresden had refused to cooperate with the Nazis?

Some groups seeking liberation say they have tried nonviolence and it has not worked, that it has brought them suffering and not liberation. And some students of social change reject nonviolence because it is "not practical." To both these groups Quakers say, "We do not ask you to chose nonviolence because it guarantees results. We have chosen it as individuals because it is the only way we can achieve peace within ourselves, even though for some of us it has been a path to suffering, and for a few, to death. We choose it because we must, and we leave the results to that Divine Spirit which we perceive as working through men and women toward unimagined ends. We do not know where the road will take us when we make our first step in the Light, but looking backward at a Fox, a Fell, a Woolman, a Mott, and others whose inner obedience has led to an impact on all of society, we say committing ourselves one by one to following the path of love may, after all, prove the most revolutionary way to change the world.''

# The Quiet Rebels

Lucretia Mott. (*Courtesy the Quaker Collection, Haverford College Library. Photo by Norman Wilson.*)

GEORGE FOX.

Founder of the Society of Friends, usually called Quakers.

George Fox, founder of the Society of Friends. (*Courtesy the Quaker Collection, Haverford College Library. Photo by Norman Wilson.*)

# Who are the Quakers?

On July 11, 1656, two women sailed into Boston Harbor aboard a small ship, the *Swallow*. Upon hearing of their arrival, the magistrates of the twenty-seven-year-old Massachusetts Bay Colony were shaken, according to a contemporary observer, "as if a formidable army had invaded their borders." Governor John Endicott being out of town, Deputy Governor Richard Bellingham took prompt, if frenzied, action. The women were held on shipboard while their boxes were searched for "blasphemous" documents. One hundred such books found in their possession were burned in the marketplace by the common hangman. The women were then transferred to prison, stripped naked and searched for tokens of witchcraft, and kept for five weeks without light or writing materials. The master of the

*Swallow* was finally ordered to transport them to Barbados and to let no person in the American colonies speak to them en route.

The two who caused all this panic looked harmless enough. Mary Fisher, a twenty-two-year-old servant girl from Yorkshire, England, and Ann Austin, a middle-aged mother of five, were members of the people called Quakers, a group recently evolved out of the religious tumult of seventeenth-century England. The threat they posed to Boston was their determination to plant the seed of their belief in the hearts of men and women in the New World. Despite the efficiency with which these first two pioneers were hustled out of town, other Quakers arrived to take their place. In a few decades, the seed was sown from Maine to South Carolina, and for a short time it seemed possible that Quakerism was to become one of the dominant religions of the colonies.

For a variety of reasons this possibility was never realized. The demanding external life of the New World had a way of distracting the Quakers from the inward experience which is the wellspring of their religious life. As they prospered, their meetings grew stodgy. To offset this they decided, around 1750, to withdraw from the world and develop themselves as a peculiar people. This move cost them much public influence, while a policy of disowning any member who married out of meeting kept their numbers small. Finally, a tragic series of schisms and separations, occurring in the nineteenth century, weakened them within and without.

The high-water mark of Quakerism in America was probably at the time of the Revolutionary War when there were 50,000 Quakers in a population of 1,580,000. Today, there are 120,000 Quakers in America, while the total population has grown to 200 million. This tiny remnant, however, continues to exercise a disproportionate influence on American life. Concepts of religious liberty and racial equality, of conscientious objection, and civil disobedience, brought by the Quakers to the colonies, are woven into the fabric of national law and custom. Early Quaker social reforms in the treatment of the Indians, the Negroes, prisoners, and the insane are still creating ripples of change. Quaker organizations such as the American Friends Service Committee are supported and staffed in part by Jews, Catholics, and Protestants who may disagree with the Quakers in many ways but share their concern to relieve the suffering of war victims and to establish the conditions of peace.

Quaker testimonies for equality and against violence grow out of a Quaker belief that "there is that of God in every man." Every person, according to Quakers, is worthy of reverence, and each has within him a seed which will illuminate his conscience and will help him to grow spiritually. When John Woolman, a Quaker abolitionist, urged southerners to free their slaves in 1757, or when the Quakers went to the Nazi Gestapo to plead for the Jews in 1938, it was in the faith that the capacity for change exists always, even in the heart of the oppressor. "Force subdues but love gains," wrote William Penn, the founder of Pennsylvania, "and he that forgives first, wins the laurel."

Although firmly rooted in Christianity, Quakerism has never had a fixed set of theological beliefs. Friends have generally felt that it is the reality of a person's religious experience that matters, not the symbols with which he tries to describe this experience. A direct experience of God is open to anyone who is willing to sit quietly and search diligently for it, Quakers believe. There are no prerequisites for this experience, neither the institution of the church, nor its sacraments, nor a trained clergy, nor even the message of the Bible, unless illuminated by the Inner Light. Every person has the capacity for religious experience, just as he has the capacity to fall in love, but he must be willing to approach worship with an open heart, experientially.

Early Quakers met in fields and in homes and later built plain meetinghouses for their worship. In its traditional form, this worship is absolutely simple. The group sits in silence for as much as an hour, during the course of which two or three worshipers may feel that they have been given a message for the others. One man speaks of a moral decision he has faced during the past week. Another quotes a favorite verse from the Bible. A woman prays for peace. Sometimes there are many messages and prayers, occasionally none. Quakers are happiest when they have a "gathered" meeting, and the same message, the same spirit, seems to have been reaching many of the worshipers at the same time.

This simple form of worship, without the benefit of trained clergy, puts the maximum responsibility upon the members of the meeting. They must discipline themselves to use the silence creatively, to be sensitive to the stirring of inspiration within the group and within themselves, to avoid the temptations of too much silence and too much speaking. The sensitivity of Quakers to social problems and the extreme democracy they practice in the conduct of the business of their meeting are closely linked to the disciplined use of silence.

But the silent meeting has its drawbacks. Unless the membership is practiced in group worship, the silence can become a void, a time of daydreaming and wool-gathering. Minutes of early Quaker meetings report the problems of members falling asleep. In the city meetings, where individual Friends had the benefits of education, travel, and varied experiences to keep them stimulated, this trend was somewhat offset, but in the small, isolated country meetings, where the exhausting work of farming left members half drugged with fatigue, the silent meetings for worship sometimes became an empty form.

During the nineteenth century, when many Quaker families joined the pioneer move to the Midwest and to the Far West, all these tendencies came to a crisis. Following an evangelical revival which swept the frontier, many Quaker meetings turned to a pastoral system and a programed meeting for worship, with hymn singing, scripture reading, and preaching. Some renamed their meetings "churches" and permitted the optional use of the sacraments.

Schisms resulting from these and other tendencies have divided the small body of American Quakers into many different groups. Today there are hymn-singing Quaker churches with a strong evangelic bent, as well as silent Quaker meetings that seem at times more philosophic than religious. The differences within the Society of Friends are probably as great as the differences between the fundamentalist Southern Baptists and the liberal Unitarians. Yet each group of Quakers goes back to the same historic sources, and each claims, with some justice, that it is following early Quaker precedent.

Quakers differ among themselves also on political and social issues. There are conservative Quaker bankers who have voted Republican all their lives, and long-haired Quaker students who demonstrate and belong to the New Left. Richard Nixon grew up as a Quaker and Staughton Lynd became one. There are probably a few Quakers in the conservative John Birch Society, as well as the liberal Americans for Democratic Action. Though the Friends are often in the news for opposition to war, many individual Quakers have served in the armed forces. Paul Douglas, a Quaker and until recently senator from Illinois, was a United States Marine. Though Friends probably agree in principle about the equality of man, they differ in the ways they act upon this belief. Some work actively to desegregate schools and neighborhoods, while others believe these changes should come slowly and naturally. More conservative Friends often are annoyed to find the Quakers in the headlines for controversial stands on peace or on race with which the whole Society is by no means in agreement.

Even if the Quakers were not divided, there would be no one body that could speak for the Society of Friends in America today. This is due to the democratic, grassroots fashion in which the Society is organized. An individual Quaker belongs to a monthly meeting, where he worships once a week and meets for business once a month. A group of monthly meetings in an area meets four times a year for quarterly meetings and a group of quarterly meetings comprise a yearly meeting. There are at present twenty-five yearly meetings in the United States, joined into three major confederations. The Friends General Conference represents primarily Eastern Friends and has a membership of 27,000; the Friends United Meeting, with headquarters in the Midwest, counts 66,000; and the Evangelical Friends Alliance in the Midwest and Far West, 23,000.

Throughout this loose structure, decisions are made not by voting but by the group as a whole reaching a common conclusion. After discussion—in a monthly meeting for example— a clerk states what he feels to be the sense of the meeting, but if a single Friend feels he cannot unite himself with the group, no decision is made. In the same fashion, a quarterly meeting will not make a decision without the support of all its member groups. The process is slow, but the miracle is that decisions are finally made.

When one asks then, "What do modern Quakers think?" or even, "Who are the Quakers?" the answer is not easy. Each Quaker group retains the right to answer for itself. But as one studies the three-hundred-year history of the Society of Friends, certain central characteristics which have had an impact on American culture emerge. To understand these, we must begin at the very beginning.

## 🌿 2
# British beginnings

Seventeenth-century England was a bubbling cauldron of religious controversy. The concept of the separation of church and state was virtually unknown. Instead, religion and politics were closely interwoven. Such events as the Guy Fawkes conspiracy and the Fifth Monarchy uprising made every new religious movement politically suspect. Public interest in religious matters was intense. Religious debates were one of the chief sources of popular entertainment and generated the excitement of a Presidential campaign or a championship boxing match.

Frightened by the Puritan doctrine of the utter depravity of man, and disillusioned by the laxity current among the Church of England clergy, more and more of the common people were turning to new religious sects. The Family of Love, which developed in the sixteenth century, believed in nonviolence and in silent worship. The Anabaptists, of the same period, rejected infant baptism, the payment of tithes, and the taking of oaths. The Seekers, coming a little later, held that the Word must be interpreted by the Spirit which inspired it, and were suspicious of a professional clergy. The Ranters, sharing many of these ideas, felt that any strong emotion was divine, and that they were above sin.

The social and economic unrest of the day gave birth to other new sects which combined religious and utopian ideas. A group called the Levellers demanded that no man be ruled by another against his will, and called for absolute social and political equality. An even more colorful sect, the Diggers, resolved to set up a democratic government based on the scriptures.

Believing that the land should be free to all, the Diggers attempted to launch their utopia by digging up and planting carrots on the common land. Established society of the day reacted to the Diggers with horror, and quickly drove them off the land. It is interesting that today among the Hippies there is a group that has taken the name of the Diggers. There are, in fact, marked similarities between the seekers of the seventeenth century and those of the twentieth. Like today's young dissidents, the Seekers, Ranters, Diggers, and Quakers rejected the built-in hypocrisy of the society of their day. Like the Hippies, they sought reality from inward experience rather than relying on outward dogmas. They did not use drugs to obtain this experience, but some of their methods of worship and of fasting produced similar states. Many were wanderers, ragged and barefoot, seeking to live communally off the land. They wore strange-looking clothes, and some had long hair and beards. The beards were particularly displeasing to the Puritans who, in the words of a Quaker observer, "made it a kind of holiness to wear short hair."

Quakerism, growing out of the same climate as many of these movements, eventually absorbed most of the people and many of the ideas. The founders of the Levellers and the Diggers, many of the Ranters, and most of the Seekers later joined the Friends. That the Quaker movement survived and flourished while the rest dwindled is perhaps due less to the uniqueness of its ideas than the uniqueness of the men who founded it. Among these the most important figure was that of George Fox.

George Fox was born in 1624 at Fenny Drayton in Leicestershire. His father, Christopher, was a weaver who had earned the nickname "Righteous Christer" for his upright behavior in the village. His mother, Mary, is said to have been of the stock of martyrs, those persecuted as dissenters in the time of Queen Mary. Not surprisingly, George grew up in this Puritan household a sober, serious child with little time or inclination for play. "If George says 'verily,' there is no altering him," the people of the village said of both his truthfulness and his obstinacy.

By the time he was eleven years old, young George began to be preoccupied by religious matters. He went faithfully to the village church, but the dichotomy between the lessons of the sermon and the ordinary behavior of the parishioners increasingly bothered him. How could a man listen to a sermon on sobriety and yet come home roaring drunk the next day? How could a woman reconcile the Bible's lessons on honesty with her proud account of shortchanging her neighbors at the market? Striving to be upright himself, he was appalled at the gap between precept and practice which he observed daily.

Although he learned to read and write and deal with simple figures, George Fox did not seem destined to be a scholar. After some debate his parents decided to apprentice him to a shoemaker, George Gee, who also kept sheep and cattle. George Fox's manual dexterity helped him become an apt pupil of the cobbler, while his love of solitude made the long hours tending the sheep, with only his Bible for company, agreeable to him. For a while it seemed he had found his niche in life.

By the time that George Fox was nineteen, he was tall, strong, and good looking, with long curling hair and very bright eyes. Instead of developing an interest in girls, however, his thoughts turned more and more to religion. He became increasingly dissatisfied with himself, his way of life, and the behavior of those around him. Well-meaning family, friends, and ministers offered advice that seemed worthless to him; such as that he take up smoking. It took only a trivial incident to galvanize his restlessness. Disillusioned one day by the behavior of a cousin who challenged him to partake in a prolonged drinking bout, he decided to leave home and wander about the country, seeking answers for his religious perplexities.

For the next four years, he traveled up and down England, talking to various preachers, meeting with various religious sects, without finding spiritual relief. The spectacle of the civil war which broke out during this time confirmed his belief that something was terribly wrong, that there must be a way to transform human life from the brutal form he saw about him to the ideal form described in the Bible. He suffered in both mind and body, frequently sleeping out in fields, fasting, enduring deep depressions as each new lead failed to produce the answers he so fervently sought.

Finally, in 1647, after he had remained alone for a long time, wandering through Derbyshire, fasting, and reading his Bible, he achieved a spiritual breakthrough, which he records in his journal:

> When all my hopes in them [the ministers he had consulted] and in all men were gone, so that I had nothing outwardly to help me, nor could tell what to do, then, oh then, I heard a

voice which said, "There is one, even Christ Jesus, that can speak to thy condition," and when I heard it my heart did leap for joy.

This was the first of many religious experiences on which George Fox based his growing faith that the Divine Spirit could speak directly to man. The scriptures he saw as the record of man's previous contact with God. But if in the time of the Old Testament, and if at the time of Jesus, then why not today? God had not once for all revealed Himself to man. There was to be a continuing revelation, as man opened his heart more and more to Christ. Nothing, neither a study of the scriptures, nor an Oxford education, nor the preaching of a learned man, was needed for this direct experience to take place.

For another five years George Fox wandered, receiving new "openings," disputing with ministers, making some converts, serving prison sentences for interrupting a church service and for blasphemy. He was still finding his way, still uncertain, and subject to moods of depression and doubt. "I also saw that there was an ocean of darkness and death, but an infinite ocean of light and love, which flowed over the ocean of darkness," he wrote in his journal. "In that I saw the infinite love of God, and I had great openings."

The Society of Friends dates its existence from 1652. In the spring of that year, George Fox came to Westmoreland and Lancashire, in the north of England, where a great group of Seekers was already in existence. After seeing a vision from on top of a mount called Pendle Hill of "a large people to be gathered," he began to make converts, not in the tens, as previously, but in the hundreds. The Seekers, who had already abandoned the "steeplehouses," the programed meetings, the sacraments, and the preachers of the time, were ready for his message. He, as a charismatic personality, galvanized their longing for direct religious experience. In turn, the responsibility of leading this large flock seems to have given George Fox a confidence and a deep commitment that remained his until his death in 1691.

It is hard to form a picture of George Fox as a person from the distance of three hundred years. His journal reveals him as sometimes harsh and vengeful, reveling in God's punishment of his enemies. Yet William Penn, a contemporary observer, says he was "a most merciful man, as ready to forgive as unapt to take or give an offense." He seems occasionally to have been driven by the compulsions of a religious fanaticism, as when he felt he must walk in stocking feet through the town of Lichfield crying, "Woe to the bloody city of Lichfield." Yet his down-to-earth, practical nature was the stabilizing factor that prevented his disciples from going to individual excess. He saw in black and white only, and he often demolished his critics with scathing tongue or pen. Yet he is described as a person of rare sweetness and warmth, who drew thousands to him and who possessed, according to Penn, a "most engaging humility and moderation."

The truth seems to be that his was a complex personality, full of contradictions which gradually became reconciled as he grew in his spiritual stature and in the exercise of leadership. Although others of his age shared many of his ideas and insights, none had the personal magnetism that drew masses to him, nor the genius for organization which resulted in the birth of so durable a religious body as the Society of Friends.

In the beginning, Fox and his followers were called Children of the Light, and they did not intend to form a new sect at all. Instead, they firmly believed that they represented the return of true, primitive Christianity and that the principle they had uncovered would be accepted everywhere and transform the world. They did not intend to limit themselves to Christendom in their outreach, for they believed that God also dwelt in the pagan, the Moslem, and the Jew.

Shortly after his experience on Pendle Hill, George Fox came to Swarthmoor Hall in Ulverston, the home of Judge Thomas Fell, his wife Margaret, and their seven children. Margaret Fell was ten years older than George Fox, but readily came under the influence of the young man's spiritual power. Her husband was never converted to Quakerism, but he permitted his home to be used as a headquarters for the movement from then on, and frequently helped Quakers in legal difficulties. Judge Fell died in 1658, and eleven years later George Fox married Margaret, who had meanwhile come increasingly to play the role of the mother of the Quaker movement.

From the newly developed center of strength in the north of England, the early Quakers went out two by two to take the Truth to all corners of the country, and to Scotland and Ireland. These "First Publishers of the Truth" are recorded in Quaker history as the "Valiant Sixty," although they numbered almost seventy men and women.

Valor was needed, for the early Quakers met persecution wherever they went. They were suspected of being secretly Catholic (a suspicion in Puritan England comparable to that of being thought an underground Communist in America during the McCarthy period), of plotting to overthrow the government, of being in league with the devil. Their doctrine of the Inner Light was misunderstood to be blasphemous, and their wandering caused them to be arrested frequently as vagrants.

The early Quakers appear to have brought some of the persecution and misunderstanding upon their own heads. They were so opposed to formal religion that they felt compelled to enter churches and call upon the congregation to forsake the "steeplehouse" and join the living church of the followers of Christ. Or they would step out onto the village green, during a country fair, and denounce the innocent revelers. The people did not always welcome these interruptions.

The Quakers did not believe any man could be made a minister by being trained at Oxford or Cambridge and hired by a congregation. They were, consequently, utterly opposed to the payment of tithes. Nor did they permit ministers to perform wedding ceremonies among them. Instead, they conducted their own weddings in a simple ceremony that continues to this day. Until this form of marriage was recognized by law, they were sometimes persecuted for living together illegally as man and wife.

Two customs which caused the Quakers great trouble in the early days were their refusal to swear oaths and to remove their hats to those in authority. The Quakers believed that Christ's injunction, "Swear not at all . . . let your communication be yea, yea, or nay, nay," should be taken literally. To swear to something suggests that a person has two standards of truth, one for everyday use and one for the times when one is under oath. As in everything else, Quakers insisted on a single standard of behavior.

Similarly, the removal of the hat to honor those in authority suggested to the early Quakers a double standard. The continental custom of hat removal was being carried to elaborate heights by the cavaliers of the period. Gentlemen made sweeping, elaborate, exaggerated bows to each other, and the poor people were expected to remove their hats to their social superiors. The Quakers wanted to emphasize that every person was the equal of every other person. Only in the presence of God, they believed, should a man remove his hat.

Over the years, Quakers have been known for their custom of using the singular "thee" and "thou" rather than the plural "you." This also represents an early witness against class distinctions. "Thee" was the commonly used second person singular in English just as the French *tu* and the German *du* are today. The custom of using "you" to refer to a single person was just being introduced by the cavaliers as a gesture of respect. Common people were supposed to address their betters as "you" just as they were supposed to remove their hats in the presence of their superiors, the lords and ladies, magistrates, or clergy.

Petty magistrates, uncertain of their own status, were particularly angered when the sturdy Quakers appeared before them and refused to accord them the honor of removing their hats and using "you." Instead, the Quakers often lectured the magistrates on their behavior. The term "Quaker" was first used when George Fox told the officials of Derby, who were in the process of charging him, that they ought "to tremble before the word of God." "You are the Quaker, not I," Judge Bennett is supposed to have said.

Since the Quakers would take no oaths at all, they naturally could not swear to the Oath of Abjuration, required after 1655 of all people to prove they were not Catholics. The Puritans saw this refusal as a definite proof of disloyalty. In addition, it put a potent weapon in the hands of local magistrates, who, angered by Quaker "insolence," sought an excuse to punish members of the sect. If all other legal devices failed, they could always produce the oath and record that the Quaker in question had refused to take it.

The Quakers' attitude toward Cromwell's New Model Army was also thought of as disloyal. When it was time for George Fox to be released from Derby prison, some officers of that army approached him and offered him the post of captain. He refused, replying that he knew "from whence all wars arose, even from the lust, according to James' doctrine," and that "I lived in the virtue of that life and power that took away the occasion of all wars." In punishment, George Fox was sent back to prison to spend six months more in a small and dirty cell.

Not all the early Quakers were pacifists. Some were soldiers in Cromwell's army before, during, and after their convincement. The Quaker peace testimony was left at first to the individual conscience. When William Penn first became a Quaker, he was still a young courtier in the court of Charles II. He is supposed to have complained to George Fox that he felt uncomfortable wearing a sword, although court custom demanded it. "Wear thy sword as long as thou canst," was Fox's rejoinder. Similarly, some Quakers stayed in Cromwell's army or navy until they were overcome by a sense of disparity between killing a man and believing that there was that of God in every man. One sailor, Thomas Lurting, recorded in his journal that he was stopped short by this thought in the very midst of loading a cannon.

Some of the Quakers in Cromwell's army got into difficulty with their superior officers over other aspects of their Quaker customs. Their refusal to show hat honor, to use the plural "you," and to take oaths caused trouble. How can you have an army, one officer complained to his superior, unless you recognize the differences of rank and station? These Quakers with their leveling attitudes will soon ruin all discipline. They must be taught a lesson.

As early as 1660, however, the Quakers as a group took a definite stand against war. Suspected of being Fifth Monarchy men, followers of a fanatic sect which believed that the Kingdom of God was about to come and should be hastened by rebellion against the present king, the Quakers presented a declaration to Charles II.

> We utterly deny all outward wars and strife and fightings with outward weapons, for any end or under any pretence whatsoever, and we do certainly know, and so testify to the world,

that the spirit of Christ, which leads us into all Truth, will never move us to fight and war against any man with outward weapons, neither for the kingdom of Christ, nor for the kingdoms of this world.

Whatever the nature of their misdemeanor in the eyes of the magistrates, Quakers were thrown into jail frequently during the first forty years of the life of the Society. Some historians estimate that 15,000 had been imprisoned by 1689, when the Act of Toleration finally was passed. In addition, there were numerous public whippings and tongue borings and brandings, as the government grew more and more anxious to stamp out the new sect.

George Fox himself was imprisoned eight times in the course of his life. The accounts of these sojourns do not make pleasant reading. The jails of the day were "nasty, stinking places" unheated in the winter, possessing no sanitary facilities, often open to the wind and the rain. Prisoners were supposed to pay the jailers for their food, and to endure whatever whippings or other punishment the jailer saw fit to inflict. There was no privacy for women, and lice were a common problem.

James Parnell, a boy of nineteen was the first Quaker to die for his new faith in prison. A harsh jailer forced him to live on a shelf high above the floor of the prison, and descend by rope for his meals. One day, weakened by hunger, he fell and broke his leg. He was then put into a cell not much larger than a baker's oven where he finally died of hunger, pain, and exhaustion. Other deaths from such mistreatment followed. In all, some 450 Quakers had perished in prison for their beliefs by 1689. At one point, 164 Quakers who were still at liberty offered to trade places with their imprisoned comrades in order to save them from death in prison. Parliament refused, but many people were deeply impressed by this willingness to sacrifice.

In 1660, shortly after the Restoration, Charles II set some

700 Quakers free, and it appeared for a short while as if the persecution would be ended. Soon, however, a special law against the Quakers was passed, followed by the Conventicle Act of 1664. Aimed at destroying all nonconforming churches, the Conventicle Act made it illegal for five or more people to assemble under the guise of worship for any service other than that of the established church. The other separatist groups met in secret, and some took food to their meetings so that if they were discovered they could pretend to be having a meal. The Quakers, however, insisted on continuing to meet openly. Hundreds were arrested and taken off to jail, but other hundreds calmly took their places. When all the adults were jailed, the children carried on. This quiet but determined acceptance of suffering affected English public opinion deeply, and, in time, contributed to the establishment of religious toleration in England.

The long years of persecution did much to weld Quakers into a cohesive group. They developed an intense loyalty and a tender concern for one another which sustained them and helped them to face joyously their many hardships.

A few, however, gave way under the strain. The most famous of these was James Nayler, a former soldier in Cromwell's army and one of George Fox's strongest supporters. After a particularly long and severe imprisonment, Nayler had an apparent breakdown. A small group of hysterical women who surrounded him insisted on addressing him as though he were a reincarnation of Jesus. Nayler permitted this and even rode into the town of Bristol while his admirers strewed garments in his path and cried "Holy, holy, holy." Found guilty of blasphemy, he was committed to the pillory, flogged through the streets of London, and branded on his forehead with "B" for blasphemer. Most painful of all, his tongue was bored with a hot iron. During a long ensuing imprisonment, he repented and was reconciled with

George Fox on his release. Several months later, setting out for Yorkshire to see his family, he was attacked by highwaymen and left dying in a field. He was found just before his death, and to those gathered about him, he is reported to have uttered some of the most beautiful words in the history of religious expression:

> There is a spirit which I feel that delights to do no evil, nor to avenge any wrong, but delights to endure all things, in hope to enjoy its own in the end. Its hope is to outlive all wrath and contention, to weary out all exaltation and cruelty, or whatever is of a nature contrary to itself. It sees the end of all temptations. As it bears no evil in itself, so it conceives of none in thoughts to any other. If it is betrayed, it bears it, for its ground and spring is the mercies and forgiveness of God. Its crown is meekness, its life is everlasting love unfeigned; it takes its kingdom with entreaty and not with contention, and keeps it by lowliness of mind.

Nayler was not the only member of the early Quaker group to become unsettled. There was an unstable element in the new movement. Converts from the Ranters and other new small sects brought with them an atmosphere of hysteria. The doctrine of the Inner Light left the way open to individual excess, since it has always been easy to confuse the promptings of hidden wishes with those of the Divine Spirit.

George Fox himself occasionally behaved erratically, and had what sound now like hysterical illnesses. Others among the early Friends felt compelled to remove all their clothes and walk through the streets of town in imitation of Isaiah. In both England and in the American colonies there were several cases of women, from young girls to grandmothers, yielding to this confused impulse. Samuel Pepys describes seeing one Quaker naked, except for a loin cloth, standing near Westminster with a platter of smoking brimstones on his head.

Nayler's defection, however, was particularly dramatic, and brought a fresh wave of persecution in its wake. George Fox's reaction was to see that it was necessary to develop some form of organization and control among the Children of the Light. In the next few years, he traveled about England and America establishing the monthly, quarterly, and yearly meeting structure that has endured to this day.

The strength of the Society of Friends for over three hundred years seems to stem from the nature of this simple organization. The individual is free to act upon his insights, but he has the group to check and counterbalance his excesses. The group in turn must nourish the freedom of the individual, or the life of the meeting flickers out. The balancing has not always worked, but when it functions it creates a serene and yet sensitive milieu.

Women were given a prominent place in the early Quaker organization. This was unusual in a society where women generally played a subordinate role and were rarely active outside the home. But the Quakers, with their belief in that of God in everyone, saw that women as well as men might be chosen by the Inner Light as ministers. At first, the business sessions of the Society were conducted by men, but women's meetings were soon established to oversee charitable activities as well as handle the problems of women members. In the meeting for worship there was no distinction from the beginning.

Despite persecution, despite the defections of unstable members, the Quaker movement continued to grow rapidly. One of its most surprising features was its ability to attract persons of all classes of society and all levels of education. George Fox was a simple shoemaker with only a rudimentary education; yet his message of direct dealings between God and man attracted several distinguished gentlemen of the age. Among these were Robert Barclay, a Scottish theologian who became the first scholarly spokesman for Quaker beliefs, and William Penn, the son of a nobleman, who founded Pennsylvania as a home for the new sect. Isaac Penington and Thomas Ellwood were others among the small band of early Quaker aristocrats.

For men such as these, becoming a Quaker demanded a complete change in their lives. Though the first Quakers did not insist upon uniformity of dress, as later generations did, they took a Puritan attitude toward brightly colored, fancy clothes, wigs, and jewelry. Like the Puritans, they distrusted art, music, and the theater. No one, Puritan or Quaker, had heard of the doctrine of total abstinence in those days, but they were opposed to excessive use of spirits and tobacco, and much given to fasting for their soul's sake. They used "thee" and "thou," referred to the days of the week as First Day, Second Day, Third Day, rather than using the pagan names Sunday, Monday, Tuesday, and to the months as First Month, Second Month, Third Month. Above all, they kept their hats on at all times except when praying. The way young Tom Ellwood's friends knew he had become a Quaker was by noting his refusal to remove his hat.

Nevertheless, there was a joyousness about the early Friends that attracted adherents. In a day of doubt and gloom, based on the growing belief in the depravity of human nature, the Quakers proclaimed a faith in the perfectibility of man through openness to the Inner Light. No one need feel lost in sin, or condemned to hell fire. As new converts came into the movement, they felt a great sense of release and a consequent lightness of spirit.

The early Quakers were young men and women, full of health, vigor, and enthusiasm. With a certain youthful ebullience, they endured persecution and kept up their efforts to make their message heard in every corner of the globe. They were great pamphleteers, pouring forth a steady stream of arguments for their faith and bitter denunciations of their critics. They were also great travelers, going up and down England, up into Scotland, across to Ireland, and over to Holland and Germany. A few Quakers reached the Mediterranean. Two, John Luffe and John Perrot, managed to see the Pope in Rome to inform him he was the Antichrist. Luffe was hanged for his pains, and Perrot committed for three years to the madhouse. At about the same time Mary Fisher, of Boston fame, somehow managed to reach Turkey and gained an audience with the Sultan. Mohammed IV, a young man of seventeen, received her courteously, and assured her that he understood every word of her message.

None of these forays outside the English-speaking world were, however, very successful. More and more the Quakers turned their faces to the New World.

# The Quakers come to the New World

The changes which swept through religious thought in England in the middle of the seventeenth century affected the New World as well. The processes of religious reformation, once launched, were self-propelling. Here and there individuals, often widely separated from one another, read their Bibles, pondered the meaning of the New Testament, and began to raise questions about the Calvinistic doctrines of the early dissenters. As a result, little groups of people with beliefs very like the Seekers formed in the new colonies.

In the Massachusetts Bay Colony, controversy swirled around the figure of Anne Hutchinson, wife of a prominent colonist and herself an outspoken and strong-minded woman. After listening to the preaching of her friend and pastor, John Cotton, Anne herself began to urge a women's group in the new colony to accept a covenant of grace, rather than a covenant of works. By this she meant that an individual could obtain salvation through a direct experience with God's grace, rather than through obeying a strict set of rules.

This belief was in direct contradiction to the doctrine of the Puritan leaders, who believed that God had revealed Himself once for all through the Holy Bible, and that salvation could be obtained only by perfect obedience to the scriptures. These founding fathers were not interested in sharing with others the religious liberty they had obtained for themselves. Instead, they were intent on creating a theocracy, a state ruled by God. The priests and magistrates, as the interpreters of God's word, were to be in charge. By exercising strict control over every aspect of the lives of the colonists, they could prevent the devil from infiltrating the new colony.

Anne Hutchinson was accordingly accused of disturbing the peace of the church, tried, and banished from the colony. With her followers she founded a colony at Portsmouth, Rhode Island, under the friendly assistance of Roger Williams. The latter, though no Seeker or Quaker in belief, had earlier quarreled with the Puritan authorities. He denied that the civil government had any valid authority over the consciences of men and he insisted that the new colonies must pay the Indians a fair price for their land. Banished, he founded a new colony at Providence, Rhode Island, for which he secured a charter in 1644.

It was the memory of these controversies which threw the magistrates into a panic when the two Quaker women, Ann Austin and Mary Fisher, arrived in July of 1656. The Bostonians had already seen how dissent could shake their colony to its roots. Yet the Quakers, they believed, were the personification of dissent and turmoil, bent on persuading their flock to desert the established church. From the Puritan point of view, this was manifestly a case of heresy and the work of the devil. When the two were searched for signs of witchcraft, the magistrates really believed that such signs would be found.

The Puritan authorities were not up against two women alone, however. Two days after Ann Austin and Mary Fisher left Boston Harbor on a ship bound for the Quaker colony on Barbados, another ship carrying eight Quakers came sailing in. At the same time there arrived a Richard Smith, of Long Island, who had been converted to Quakerism on a trip to the home country in 1654, and was perhaps the first American Quaker.

The members of this second invasion were held while their belongings were searched for "erroneous books and hellish pamphlets," examined by the Boston ministers, and thrown into jail for eleven weeks. At the end of this time, the master of the vessel which had brought them was compelled to take them straight back to England under a five-hundred-pound bond. Richard Smith was sent home to Long Island by sea, lest he meet and infect any travelers on a land journey.

Taking no chances with a third invasion, the general court of Massachusetts passed a law against Quakers while these eight were still in jail. Any master of a sailing vessel bringing a Quaker into the colony was to be fined one hundred pounds, and anyone owning or concealing a Quaker book was to pay five pounds. Any Quaker brash enough to return to the colony would be arrested, whipped, committed to the house of correction,

kept constantly at work, prevented from having conversation
with anyone until he was safely out of the colony.

At least one citizen of Boston objected, however. Old Nicholas
Upsall, a town father, had taken pity on Ann Austin and Mary
Fisher and arranged with the jailer for them to have extra rations
at his expense. When the new anti-Quaker law was proclaimed
through the streets of Boston, he stood on his doorstep and raised
his voice in protest. For this he was brought before the court,
fined, and banished. He spent the winter of 1656 in Sandwich
and went on to Rhode Island in the spring, suffering many
hardships on the way. The Indians befriended him and were
horrified at the way he had been treated. "What a God have the
English who deal so with one another over the worship of their
God," a chief is said to have commented.

For a time, it appeared as though the new law against Quakers
was going to be effective. Shipmasters were afraid to take
Quakers to Boston, and many who wished to sail to the New
World were denied passage. This situation did not last long
however. Robert Fowler, a Quaker convert from Bridlington,
England, felt under divine guidance to build a ship and sail to
America. He had, so far as we know, no previous experience,
and the ship he built, the *Woodhouse*, was far too small for an
ocean voyage. Nevertheless, Fowler was confident that God
would guide it, just as He did the Ark. In the middle of June,
1657, the little ship set to sea with eleven Quakers aboard.
With no navigational instruments, they depended entirely on
divine guidance to set their course, holding meetings for worship whenever they felt unsure of how to set their sails. Despite
three major storms at sea, they arrived safely early in August
in the creek between the Dutch Plantations and Long Island. Five
members of the group here went ashore to visit New Amsterdam,
while the remaining six sailed on. They endured the worst

hazards of their voyage coming through Hell Gate but crossed safely into Long Island Sound, and finally reached Newport, Rhode Island, after six weeks of sailing.

Though Anne Hutchinson was now dead, her followers were ready to receive the Quaker message. Mary Dyer, a friend of Anne's, had just returned from a trip to England where she had become a convinced Friend. Landing in Boston, she had been thrown in jail for her new beliefs. Now back in Rhode Island, she served as the nucleus for the formation of a new Quaker group. Convincements followed quickly upon the landing of the *Woodhouse* group. Soon other New England colonies were warning Rhode Island to get rid of the dangerous Quaker doctrine spreading within the colony. In ringing words, Rhode Island refused to do this: "We have no law among us whereby to punish any for only declaring by words their minds and understandings concerning the things and ways of God, as to salvation and an eternal condition. . . ." Thus the Quakers were assured of a haven in the New World.

The *Woodhouse* Argonauts did not, however, tarry in their haven. They had been sent, they felt, to plant the seed in the Massachusetts Bay Colony, and they could not rest until they had done so. One of their members, Mary Clark, went straight to Boston where she received a severe whipping and twelve weeks of solitary confinement. Christopher Holder and John Copeland felt guided to go to Martha's Vineyard. Here the white settlers met them with hostility, but the Indians befriended them and helped them sail to the Massachusetts mainland. In both Sandwich and Plymouth the two made Quaker converts, throwing the officials of the church and the town into a fury. At length they were escorted out of town, but they had scarcely left before another *Woodhouse* passenger, Humphrey Norton, took their place. He, too, made convincements and he, too, was hustled away by the frantic town officials. Even this didn't stop the Quakers; a third missionary, William Brend, promptly arrived in the colony and helped to found a thriving meeting in the town of Scituate.

The Puritans attempted to meet the rising tide of Quakerism as best they could, sometimes by force, sometimes by persuasion. In 1659, the General Court of Plymouth sent Isaac Robinson and three others to attend the Quaker meetings and to "reduce them from the error of their ways." Instead, Robinson himself was convinced, and left Plymouth to found a new Quaker settlement at Falmouth.

In Salem a small group of persons with views like the Seekers had already formed and were meeting in the home of Lawrence and Cassandra Southwick, "a grave and aged" couple with grown children. Samuel Shattuck, another member of this group, and the Southwicks were present when John Copeland and Christopher Holder attended the Puritan Salem Meeting. After the sermon, Holder attempted to speak a few words. Infuriated, one of the church members seized him by the hair and stuffed a glove and a handkerchief into his mouth. He would have choked to death if Samuel Shattuck had not intervened. For befriending the Quakers in this fashion, Shattuck and the Southwicks were sent to Boston for punishment. Lawrence Southwick was turned over to the church authorities, and Samuel Shattuck was placed under bond not to go to any more Quaker meetings, but Cassandra Southwick was imprisoned for seven weeks for having a Quaker paper in her possession. The two British Quakers were beaten with a three-knotted whip and placed in an unheated prison for nine weeks.

Nevertheless, the Quaker tide continued to swell. In Lynn and in Providence new convincements followed quickly upon each other. Despite beatings and imprisonments, some of them extremely cruel, the Quaker missionaries continued to sow the seed.

In October of 1657, the Massachusetts Bay Colony passed a new and stricter law, inflicting a fine of one hundred pounds on any man who brought a Quaker into the colony, forty shillings an hour for every hour one should entertain or conceal a Quaker. Quakers returning to the colony after once being banished were to have their ears cropped and their tongues bored with a hot iron.

These threats seemed only to increase the Quaker zeal to go to the lion's den, as they called Boston. By August of 1658, three Quakers had returned and each had lost an ear. In desperation, the Boston authorities passed a final law. Any convicted of being Quakers should be banished from the colony on pain of death. The small group of Quakers in Salem was broken up and its members fined and deported. The aged Southwicks went to Shelter Island, where they died shortly afterward. When their grown children, left in Salem, could not pay their parents' fines, the authorities made an effort to sell them into slavery. Fortunately, no shipmaster could be found willing to execute such an order. Other Quakers from Salem went to Barbados and back to England. For a year after the passage of the new law there was a period of apparent calm. Then its final clause was put to the test.

On the State House grounds opposite Boston Common today stands the statue of Mary Dyer, Quaker, with the inscription, "Witness for Religious Freedom. Hanged on Boston Common, 1660." Mary was one of four Quakers to lose their lives between October, 1659, and March, 1661, in defiance of the Boston laws. Much like the civil rights leaders of the present generation, they were drawn to defy a law which they regarded as unjust. "We go into the lion's den to look their bloody laws in the face," they wrote. Against growing public unrest, the court insisted upon carrying out the death sentence on the stubborn Quakers.

William Robinson and Marmaduke Stephenson, hanged on October 27, 1659, were English Quakers who had come to the New World under missionary fervor. William Leddra, hanged March 14, 1661, was a member of the small Quaker group in Barbados. Mary Dyer, however, may properly be considered an American. In 1635, as a bride of eighteen, she accompanied her older Separatist husband in a voyage to the New World and settled in Boston. Here she became a friend of Anne Hutchinson, and when the latter was banished, the Dyers were among those to set up a new colony on Aquidneck Island, the present-day Portsmouth. A year later, as a result of quarrels in the little colony, a small group including the Dyers broke off to form a new settlement in Newport.

There followed many serene years, in which Mary Dyer devoted herself to her husband and her large family of children. She was a warm and happy person, but she was increasingly troubled by the doctrines of Calvinism. When she returned to England with her husband and children in 1652 to visit her aged mother, she was ripe for the Quaker message. A year later she was convinced and spent many months traveling up and down England with the First Publishers of the Truth.

Returning to Boston in 1657, she was thrown into jail under the newly created anti-Quaker laws. Though she was shortly released on bond to her husband, this experience stayed with her and haunted her reunion with her children and her friends. Eventually she felt compelled to return to Boston again, and then again, until at last she was condemned to die.

To the magistrates of Boston, Mary Dyer wrote a final epistle which has long been remembered:

> In love and meekness I beseech you to repeal these cruel laws, to stay this wicked sentence. . . . But if one of us must die that others may live, let me be the one; for if my life were freely granted by you, I could not accept it so long as my sisters

Mary Dyer. (*Courtesy Earlham College. Statue by Sylvia Shaw Judson. Photo by Susan Castator.*)

suffered and my brothers died. For what is life compared with the witness of truth.

On October 27, 1659, she was sent to the gallows with two others, blindfolded, and the rope placed around her neck. Then at the last minute she was reprieved and placed in the custody of her husband. The officials of Boston hoped to frighten her into submission by this action. They did not succeed. On May 21, 1660, she returned to Boston, and on June 1 she was hanged.

"She hangs there like a flag," a local citizen said in jest. In actual fact her death became a flag, a symbol of religious liberty.

Though many Quakers were regularly imprisoned in England, none were executed. Alarmed by the deaths of their brothers and sisters in New England, English Quakers appealed to Charles II to intervene. "There is a vein of innocent blood opened in thy dominion which will run over all if it is not stopped," Edward Burroughs told his sovereign. "But I will stop that vein," the King replied. He prepared a mandamus on the spot, and with fine irony, entrusted it to Samuel Shattuck, the Salem Quaker who had been banished on pain of death.

The arrival of the King's missive provided a moment of triumph for the New England Quakers and their sympathizers. Samuel Shattuck, upon reaching Boston, demanded to see the governor himself, and was ushered into his presence wearing his hat. In anger, John Endicott ordered the servants to remove the hat. Shattuck then produced his credentials as a royal messenger and showed the mandamus. The governor at once recovered and ordered the Quaker's hat to be given back to him. He read the missive and announced laconically, "We shall obey his Majesty's commands." He then ordered all the Quakers at present in custody to be released.

Even before the receipt of the King's missive, the magistrates had been forced by public opinion to abandon the death penalty as a means of curbing the Quakers. Frightened of heresy as they were, the men and women of the Massachusetts Bay Colony could not stomach the hanging of their defenseless fellow citizens. At each whipping and each hanging more and more individuals found the courage to speak out against the brutal practices, while the common people rallied to provide the Quakers with food and clothing. It was, some say, the first successful demonstration of the power of nonviolence to move the hearts of the people against oppression.

Nevertheless, the magistrates were by no means finished. Instead of the death penalty they passed the Cart and Whip Act, under which any banished Quakers who returned would be tied to the end of a cart and whipped through town. Under the provisions of this act, several of the prisoners who were released by order of the King's missive were whipped before they left the colony. The next year, three women who visited the present territories of New Hampshire and Maine were ordered stripped to the waist and were whipped through the length of eleven towns: Dover, Hampton, Salisbury, Newbury, Rawley, Ipswich, Wenham, Lynn, Boston, Roxbury, and Dedham.

Whippings and imprisonments continued to be the lot of the Quakers in New England until the death of John Endicott in March, 1665. In May of that year, the Royal Commissioners commanded the General Court of Massachusetts to allow the Quakers to attend to their secular business without further interference. There was a lull in persecution until 1675 when the Boston Colony proclaimed a Day of Humiliation for its recent sins: neglect to teach the young, wearing of long hair, and neglect to suppress the Quakers and their meetings! These sins, according to the Puritans, had brought the wrath of God down upon them in the form of the Indian wars. To rectify the situation a new law was enacted imposing a fine on any person who attended a Quaker meeting. This law was enforced for two years, then dropped. Twenty-one years after the arrival of the *Swallow*, Friends were at last allowed to go about their business in Massachusetts.

Meanwhile, Quaker missionaries were visiting the other colonies of the New World and meeting similar persecution as a result of their zeal. The Quaker invasion of New York began with the landing of five passengers from the *Woodhouse*. They may have expected a tolerant reception since the proprietors of the New Netherlands had expressly directed that all forms of religion should be tolerated in the colony. Instead, Governor Peter Stuyvesant was almost as upset by their arrival as the magistrates of Boston. Two local ministers wrote the authorities in Amsterdam a revealing account of this event:

> On August 16th (or 12th) a ship came from the sea to this place having no flag flying from the topmast, nor any from any other part of the ship. They fired no salute from the fort. When the master of the ship came on shore and appeared before the Director General, he rendered him no respect, but stood with his hat firm on his head as if he was a goat. . . . At last information was gained that it was a ship with Quakers aboard. . . . We supposed they went to Rhode Island for that is the receptacle of all sorts of riff-raff people and is nothing else than the sewer of New England. They left behind two strong young women. As soon as the ship departed, these women began to quake and go into a frenzy, and cry out loudly in the middle of the street that men should repent, for the Day of Judgment was at hand. Our people, not knowing what was the matter, ran to and fro while one cried "fie" and another something else. The Fiscal seized them both by the head and led them to prison.

After eight days the two women, Mary Weatherhead and Dorothy Waugh, were sent with their hands tied behind them to Rhode Island. Meanwhile, the other three who made up the party —Robert Hodgson, Richard Doudney, and Sarah Gibbons—

made a trip into Long Island. Around Gravesend, Jamaica, and Hempstead they found a group of Seekers who had moved to Long Island to escape New England's Puritanism. The leader of the group was a woman known as Lady Deborah Moody. Like the followers of Anne Hutchinson's group on Rhode Island, the Moody group was ready for the Quaker message and greeted the *Woodhouse* voyagers warmly. After a short visit, Richard Doudney and Sarah Gibbons went on to Rhode Island, leaving Robert Hodgson behind for a longer stay.

Stuyvesant's men were meanwhile searching for the wandering three. They found Robert Hodgson at Hempstead, tied him to the tail of a cart, and marched him all the way to the Brooklyn Ferry. In New Amsterdam he was tried and sentenced to hard labor at a wheelbarrow for two years. When he refused to obey this sentence he was beaten and thrown back into prison. The liberty-loving Dutch of Manhattan objected to this treatment and finally persuaded Governor Stuyvesant to set the Quaker free and send him to Rhode Island.

This was not the end of the story. As the Quaker movement grew on Long Island, the governor felt more and more exercised about suppressing the supposed heresy. An anti-Quaker act with fines and punishment similar to those enacted by Massachusetts was finally passed in 1658. At the same time an old law against conventicles was revived. Henry Townsend of Flushing was the first person to suffer under this campaign. He was heavily fined for allowing his house to be used as a conventicle or gathering place, and when he refused to pay his fine, he was imprisoned and beaten. The inhabitants of Flushing, though not all Quakers, were angry about his treatment, and gathered to publish a remonstrance against this invasion of their liberties. The Flushing Remonstrance is still remembered as an early statement of the rights of conscience.

Though the authorities of New Amsterdam penalized the signers of the remonstrance and the town itself, and elsewhere did what they could to prevent Quaker meetings, the movement continued to spread. By 1659, there were regular meetings at Setauket, Oyster Bay, Hempstead, and Gravesend. Westbury and Matinecock followed a few years later. In 1662, four citizens of Barbados bought Shelter Island and made it a sanctuary for the Quakers. By the payment of one hundred and fifty pounds, half in beef and half in pork, the owners got the island exempted forever from military taxes and military duty.

The struggle for freedom of conscience on Long Island came to a climax with the arrest of John Bowne of Flushing. Fined for allowing his house to be used for a conventicle, Bowne was threatened with banishment from the colony if he did not pay his fine. Naturally he refused, and three months later the authorities angrily sent him back to Amsterdam. When Bowne presented his case to the Directors of the Dutch West India Company, they were indignant and sent a strong letter back to Governor Stuyvesant:

> It is our opinion that . . . the consciences of men ought to remain free and unshackled. Let every one remain free as long as he is modest, moderate, and his political conduct is irreproachable.

Governor Stuyvesant bowed to these wishes of his employers and left the Quakers alone. The next year, when the colony was taken over by the British, religious liberty was guaranteed. Quakers thereafter were never persecuted as a matter of policy, though there were a few sporadic attempts to suppress the group, and occasional trouble about their refusal to pay tithes or to support the militia.

In New England and New York the Quakers were feared as

the bearers of heresy. In the southern colonies they were mistrusted as enemies of the established church and state. It is of course true that they were opposed to the organized religions of the day. They bore no witness against the state as such, but certain of their practices appeared to public officials as distinct threats. These included their unwillingness to take oaths or to render hat honor to officials, and their way of creating public commotions.

The first pioneer to arrive in the southern colonies was Elizabeth Harris, who visited Virginia and Maryland in 1656 at about the same time as Mary Fisher and Ann Austin arrived in Boston. The next year, two Quakers from England, Josiah Coale and Thomas Thurston, spent six months in Virginia and a shorter time in Maryland before pushing on through virgin forest to New England. Three of the *Woodhouse* crew arrived in 1658 to continue the work of planting the seed.

Virginia was not slow to react to the coming of the Quakers. In the spring of 1660 the Act for Suppressing the Quakers was passed, which reveals the way in which the Children of the Light appeared:

> Whereas there is an unreasonable and turbulent sort of people commonly called Quakers, who, contrary to the law, do daily gather together unto them assemblies and congregations of the people, teaching and publishing lies ... attempting thereby to destroy religion, lawes, communities, and all bonds of civil societies ... it is enacted that no master of a ship do bring into this colonie any person or persons called Quakers under penalty of 100 pounds. ...

In 1662, a second law fining Quakers for nonattendance at church and for unlawful assemblies was passed, and later in the same year informers were offered half the fine of two thousand pounds of tobacco for giving the authorities the names of persons who refused to have their children baptized.

Since Quakers steadfastly refused to pay these fines, many were imprisoned. One man, George Wilson, was so severely treated that he died in a Jamestown prison. Nevertheless, the group continued to grow. A large community of Quakers lived for many years in Lower Norfolk County, along the Elizabeth River. In the eighteenth century their numbers were increased by Friends from Pennsylvania and Maryland who moved south, settling in Hopewell, Fairfax, and Lynchburg. Persecution of Friends as such ended by 1680, although trouble about tithing continued until the Bill of Rights was adopted at the beginning of the Revolutionary War.

Even in Maryland, famous for its religious toleration, the Quakers were mistrusted. The first entry about Quakers in the Colonial Records of Maryland, dated 1658, expressed "alarm" over "the increase of the Quakers" and reports that Thomas Thurston and Josiah Coale were imprisoned for refusal to take an oath. Later entries refer to other imprisonments and whippings of Quakers. This reaction seems to have been based less on bigotry than on the fear that the Quakers actually were revolutionaries, determined to undermine the civil government. As the Quakers increased, this fear lessened, and the Children of the Light were able to settle to a peaceful existence.

In 1671, an Irish Quaker, William Edmundson, with two companions, started south from Virginia into what is now North Carolina. It was, he writes in his journal, "All wilderness and no English inhabitants or padways, only some marked trees to guide people." After several days of wandering, they came to the house of Henry Phillips on the Albemarle River. Phillips and his wife had become convinced Quakers in New England seven years earlier and had moved to North Carolina to escape persecution. At the time of Edmundson's arrival, they had not seen a Quaker for seven years. They wept for joy and would have provided warm food and a bed for the weary travelers,

but Edmundson insisted that they invite their frontier neighbors
to a meeting that very day. These frontiersmen had little or no
religion, but they received the Quaker message warmly. Edmundson left behind a small nucleus of convinced Friends
which subsequently grew to be a thriving Quaker community.

Throughout the eighteenth century Quakers continued to
increase in the population of North Carolina. In the 1730's,
Friends from Pennsylvania and Maryland began to move into
the colony, and in the 1750's a large group of young Quaker
men moved south from overcrowded Quaker Nantucket Island.
They settled in the New Garden Meeting area, the home of
Guilford College today. Other Nantucketeers moved into South
Carolina and Georgia, but Quakerism never flourished in the
latter colonies, and the meetings they established soon vanished.

The planting of the seed in the New World, as the Quakers
termed it, was vastly aided by the visits of traveling missionaries,
like William Edmundson. Others—John Burnyeat, Thomas
Chalkley, John Richardson, David Sands, John Fothergill—
helped to spread the Word from Maine to Georgia. These men
traveled great distances through the wilderness, often sleeping
on the cold ground in the middle of the winter, and swimming
their horses through deep rivers, in order to bring the Word
to new converts, and to link up little Quaker groups with one
another. George Fox himself traveled throughout the colonies
for two years, from 1671 to 1673.

Nurtured by the visits of these Public Friends, new meetings
were formed and older meetings continued to grow throughout
the colonies. Quakerism grew in Maine and New Hampshire,
throughout Massachusetts and in Rhode Island. The Island of
Nantucket became a Quaker stronghold. A string of meetings
developed between the present state of Connecticut and New
York: Mamaroneck, Westchester, Purchase, New Milford, and

Nine-Partners among them. The Quaker movements continued to expand on Long Island and along the southern seaboard. First New Jersey, and then Pennsylvania became the site of mass Quaker settlements.

As the Quakers grew in strength they began to play a role in public life. In North Carolina, where Quakerism was the only organized religion for many years, a Quaker governor, John Archdale, was chosen and a number of Friends elected to the Assembly. The colony, enjoying good relations with the Indians, prospered under Quaker rule until 1704. In that year Parliament passed a new act requiring an oath of allegiance to Queen Anne. The North Carolina Friends, unable to take the oath, were thrown out of office.

In Rhode Island, where the Quakers were actually in the majority, the Friends held important public posts for over a hundred years. For thirty-six of these years, a Quaker governor ruled the colony. It was the first time that the Friends had a chance to test their principles against the demands of public responsibility, and it was not entirely a success. The English colonies were sporadically engaged in war with the Dutch or with the Indians during these years, and the Rhode Island Quaker governors had the choice of violating their pacifist convictions by joining in these struggles on the demand of the home government, or of losing their charter. Rather than sticking by an absolute position, they chose to compromise. They were often under attack from their own people for this failure to live up to Quaker principles, while the non-Quaker residents of Rhode Island, and the home government, constantly complained that they were not warlike enough.

They were, however, widely regarded as good governors. And though they compromised to the extent of raising a militia at the demand of the King, they managed to enact one aspect of

Quaker belief into law. They wrote the first exemption for those of "tender" conscience:

> Be it therefore enacted, and hereby it is enacted by his Majesty's authority, that noe person (within this Collony) that is or hereafter shall be persuaded in his conscience that he cannot or ought not to trayne, to learne to fight, nor to war, nor to kill any person or persons, shall at any time be compelled against his judgment and conscience to trayne, arm, or fight, to kill any person or persons by reason of or at the command of any officer of this Collony, civil or military, nor by reason of any by-law here past or formerly enacted, nor shall suffer any punishment, fine, distraint, penalty, nor imprisonment, who cannot in conscience trayne, fight or kill any person, or persons for the aforesaid reasons.

As the seventeenth century came to an end, change became apparent in the Quaker community, both in England and in the colonies. The First Publishers of the Truth, young men and women in the 1650's, were dying off, leaving in their place a new generation which had not participated in the excitement of the early movement. One of the weaknesses of the Quaker religion through the years has been the assumption that the children of Friends would automatically share in the fruits of the religious experience of their parents. The fact that there is little reliance within the classic tradition of Quakerism on religious education leaves the transmission of values entirely in the hands of the individual family and meeting. It does not always work. In the case of the second generation of Quakers, sons and daughters seemed to inherit the intense group loyalty which outside persecution had developed among their parents, but to lack the radiant outgoing spirit which had made these first Friends missionaries advance to the far corners of the earth.

It was in part a natural reaction to rejection. The First Publishers had been thoroughly rebuffed by what seemed to them a hostile world. They and their children could only conclude that perhaps the world was not yet ready to receive the seed. Instead, they must keep themselves carefully separate from a world that was out of joint, and pass their principle on from generation to generation until the times were ripe for their message.

Some of the enthusiasm that had gone in the early years into the transmission of the message was now turned by the latter-day Quakers into policing of their own membership. In the past, the excess enthusiasm and instability of some of their members had brought suffering down upon the whole group. Now it seemed important to keep all who called themselves Quakers in line. The overseers of the meeting began to exercise an increasing control over the members, and the policy of disowning those who did not live up to the Quaker testimonies began.

As the movement slowly became a sect, growing attention was given to the organization of meetings, to the care of the sick, the poor, and the widowed, to deepening the bonds between little groups of Friends. Monthly and quarterly meetings were often held in the homes of local Quakers. The quarterly meetings were partially social gatherings, lasting for several days. Intervisitation was kept up by traveling ministers, or Public Friends, and by the constant exchange of letters and gifts. In 1678 there is a recorded minute of concern under which the women Friends of Maryland sent the women Friends of London two hogsheads of tobacco.

The meeting's concern for the life of the individual member encompassed every part of it. For the children of the meeting, small schools providing a guarded rudimentary education were established. Young people ready to marry were visited and their marriages allowed only if the overseers of the meeting regarded them as "clear." Men were advised in regard to the honesty and thrift with which they pursued a livelihood. Friends were asked not to carry their quarrels into the courts of the world's people but to settle them within the meeting.

A few minutes chosen from early monthly meetings illustrate this breadth of involvement:

> At a men and women Meeting in ye house of Matthew Prior at Matinecock it was agreed on in ye Meeting that such as could find anything upon them shall go unto Dorety Farington of Flushing and speake unto her in love and in ye meekness to know whether she will owne judgment for her walking and acting contrary unto ye truth in taking a husband of ye world and not in unity of Friends.

> Our Friend Tarlton Woodson having related to this Meeting his case of having had a horse wrongfully seazed by the sheriff for a Melishy [militia] fine, for not bearing arms according as the Law directs, and desires of this Meeting advice whether he may sew [sue] the said auficer for not acting according to Law. This Meeting after deliberate concideration think it may redound more to the honor of Truth to suffere wrong patiently than to take a remedy at Law.

> The overseers are informed that there is a bad report concerning two members salting up beef and exposing it for sale, which was not merchantable; and they have made some inquiry, and do not find things clear, therefore this Meeting appoints a committee to make inquiry.

Friends were exceedingly concerned about their reputation for truthfulness. So much so that they developed early the habit of understatement. There is a story, perhaps apocryphal, of two Quakers passing a field in which some recently shorn sheep were grazing.

"Friend, I see these sheep have been shorn," the younger Quaker said.

"Well at least they have been shorn on the side facing the road," the older Quaker replied.

This carefulness about the truth soon earned them their reputation of being honest tradesmen. In a day when haggling was still everywhere used, they introduced the concept of the fixed price. When a Quaker said his price was four shillings, it was four shillings, and nothing could sway him. As a result people began to feel that they could trust the Quaker merchants above others, and their business grew. In England both the professions and government service were closed to Quakers because of their refusal to take oaths. Instead they entered the developing wool and cloth trades, banking, and, strange to say, brewing. Their diligence and thrift and sobriety soon made them wealthy. In the American colonies, they were also prosperous farmers and whalers.

As a mark of their growing sense of separateness, the second generation of Quakers began to dress in a distinct fashion, to wear the Quaker gray, the broad-brimmed hat and the Quaker bonnet, which were to set them apart for many years. The early Quaker pioneers had worn no such uniform and some were appalled by this new development. Just before her death in 1702, Margaret Fell commented on the developing custom. "We must look at no colors, nor make anything that is changeable colors as the hills are, nor sell them nor wear them. But we must be all in one dress and one color. This is a silly poor Gospel."

Nevertheless, the "silly poor Gospel" prevailed. As Quakers grew wealthy, they developed the habit of buying the very best, though the plainest goods that money could obtain. For years, Quaker linen meant the highest grade of linen available in the colonies. There are minutes of Quaker meetings dealing with members whose dress was not sufficiently somber, and records of long discussions on the size of lapels.

Some of the early Quakers were brewmasters. The testimony against the use of alcohol which came to be regarded as characteristic of Quakers did not become current until the nineteenth century. Early Quakers, like all their contemporaries, drank ale and beer and believed a little rum was needed to get through the winter months. They objected to intoxication, however, and dealt with any of their members who showed signs of overindulging.

The meeting, fortunately, did not devote itself only to negative regulation even in this first period of retrenchment. It warmly supported its members who developed a gift for the ministry, or a sense of mission to visit other meetings, or a concern for the righting of a social evil. As the realization that slavery was in opposition to their faith deepened among American Quakers, they reminded members to free themselves of this institution; first of being involved in the slave trade, later of holding slaves at all.

The most striking aspect of the life of the Quakers in the American colonies was their good relations with the Indians. These good relations prevailed from Maine to Georgia. In those colonies where the Quakers held political power—Rhode Island, Pennsylvania, New Jersey, and North Carolina—there were practically no border raids or Indian uprisings. In other colonies, where the Indians felt themselves to have been cheated and ousted by sharp settlers, the Quakers were able to live peacefully in their frontier settlements, unharmed by Indian war parties.

The secret of these good relations was a simple one. While many of the other settlers believed that the Indians were heathen savages, the Quakers saw them as children of God, and treated them with consequent respect. According to Calvinist doctrine of the time, man without God was utterly depraved, therefore nothing but depravity could be expected of the pagan Indian. According to the Quaker, every man bore within him an inner teacher, whether or not he had had the opportunity to learn about the life and teachings of Jesus.

Fox was visiting a few scattered Friends in Albemarle County, North Carolina, in 1672 when a doctor staying there at the Governor's House

> would needs dispute . . . concerning the light and spirit of God which he denied to be in everyone; and affirmed that it was not in the Indians.
>
> Whereupon I called an Indian to us, and asked him whether when he lied or did wrong to anyone there was not something in him that reproved him for it. He said that there was such a thing in him, that did so reprove him, and he was ashamed when he had done wrong, or spoken wrong.

The Quakers insisted that the Indian be treated like the white man, that his land be purchased rather than taken from him, that he have trials by jury composed of Indians and white men, and that his grievances be arbitrated at a time of dispute. They generally also refrained from the prevalent custom of turning captive Indians into slaves. Other settlers also paid the Indians for their lands, but the Quakers were apparently the most consistent on this score. As a result, the Indians came to trust the Quakers. There were several instances when an Indian tribe refused to sign a treaty with the white men unless a Quaker was there to witness the deed.

In turn, the Quakers trusted the Indians. They did not, like their neighbors, rush into garrisons when there were rumors of Indian troubles. Instead, they remained on their farms, worked in the fields without firearms, and left the latchstring out at night. Only a handful of Quakers were ever harmed by the

Indians, and most of these, according to early records, were those who had given way to a "slavish fear."

Thomas Story, a prominent Quaker missionary, tells of two young Friends walking together, one with a gun and one without.

> The Indians shot him who had the gun, but hurt not the other. And when they knew the young man they had killed was a Friend, they seemed sorry for it, but blamed him for carrying a gun, for they knew the Quakers would not fight nor do them any harm, and therefore, by carrying a gun, they took him for an enemy.

Among these early records are other remarkable stories of this nature: young couples leaving their children with the Indians while they journeyed to quarterly meetings; Quakers traveling unarmed into hostile Indian territory when the Indians were on the warpath; an Indian war party with many scalps coming into a Quaker meeting for worship on the frontier, and slipping quietly out again so as not to disturb the worshipers.

When Quakers objected to giving money and raising a militia for the various frontier wars that plagued the new American colonies, they were justified in arguing that if the colonies were to adopt a better policy toward the Indians, there would indeed be no war. As a matter of fact, for over seventy years there was peace between the settlers of Pennsylvania and their Indian neighbors. This was perhaps the most successful single outcome of the not always successful Holy Experiment.

# 4

# The Holy Experiment

And thou, Philadelphia, the virgin settlement of this province, named before thou wert born, what love, what care, what service and what travail have there been to bring thee forth and preserve thee from such as would abuse and defile thee.
—WILLIAM PENN

The idea of establishing a home for the persecuted Quakers of England somewhere in the New World occurred to George Fox and his followers early in the development of the Quaker movement. In 1660 one of the traveling Friends, Josiah Coale, was instructed to visit the Indians of the Susquehanna and discuss the purchase of lands. Although this first venture came to nothing, interest in the scheme did not die.

To young William Penn, an aristocratic convert to Quakerism, the thought of establishing a Quaker colony had special appeal. Not only would such a venture provide a refuge for Quakers, he reasoned, it would also give the world a demonstration of how Quakerism, freed from hampering restrictions, could work to transform the whole life of a people. A student of both religion and government, he became increasingly eager to find a way to make this "Holy Experiment."

In 1674, West Jersey was purchased by two Quakers who promptly quarreled over the division of the land. Young Penn was asked to arbitrate. A complicated legal struggle ensued, resulting eventually in the bankruptcy of both men. Penn, as a creditor, became one of three Quaker proprietors of West Jersey. A few years later East Jersey was turned over to twelve proprietors, one of them, again, William Penn.

Quaker settlement in West Jersey was rapid. In 1675, a group of Quakers sailed from England in a ship called the *Griffin* and founded a colony at Salem. Two years later a second ship, the *Kent,* brought a group to the site of the city of Burlington. Within eighteen months, eight hundred Quakers had arrived, and by 1681 there were fourteen hundred in the new province.

Even before the first settlers arrived, the owners had published the "Concessions" under which they proposed to govern. Though the document is anonymous, undoubtedly Penn helped to write it. The new charter proclaimed religious liberty, an assembly elected by the people, and trial by jury, all elements to be found later in Penn's famous Frame of Government.

> We have made concessions by ourselves [Penn and his partners wrote] being such as Friends here and there (we Question not) will approve of. . . . There we lay a foundation for after ages to understand their liberty as men and Christians, that they may not be brought in bondage but by their own consent, for we put the power in the people.

At the time of his involvement in the settling of New Jersey, Penn was a young man in his thirties, already prominent in the Society of Friends and in the court of the English kings. The son of Sir William Penn, an admiral in the King's navy, young Penn was educated at Oxford, but expelled for his dissenter sympathies. His father next sent him to L'Académie Protestante de Saumur in France to study for a year. After this he was dispatched to Ireland to manage the family estates. Years before, when a boy of twelve, Penn had been to Ireland with his father and had been deeply affected by hearing a Quaker, Thomas Loe, speak. Now back in Ireland, he decided to look the Quakers up. As a result he became a Friend and returned to England to face the anger of his father and a series of arrests and imprisonments for his new views.

Penn was a great addition to the young Society of Friends from the outset. A prolific and eloquent writer, he took the Quaker position in several of the religious pamphlet wars of the day, scribbling defenses of the Quakers both while he was in prison and out. His gift for the law was also a great help. Hat firmly on his head, he appeared before magistrates time without number to plead the Quaker cause.

In 1670, he and a friend, William Meade, were arrested for attending a meeting for worship in Gracechurch Street, in defiance of the recently passed Conventicle Act. In the ensuing trial the judge charged the jury to bring in a verdict of guilty, and when they refused to do so, ordered them imprisoned. "You are Englishmen; mind your privileges, give not away your right!" Penn called to the jury. The twelve jurors stood their ground, and after they were released won suit against the judges. The case was long remembered as one establishing the inviolability of trial by jury.

In addition to his abilities as a writer and a legal advocate, Penn was an able religious leader. In 1671, 1677, and again in 1686, he traveled in Holland and Germany, visiting the little Quaker groups that were forming in such sites as Amsterdam and Krisheim. In England, and later in Pennsylvania, Friends flocked to meeting when Penn was in attendance. Some of his devotional writing such as "No Cross, No Crown" became famous in religious literature. As he grew older his spiritual gifts deepened.

In 1671, Penn married Gulielma Springett, daughter of Mary Penington and stepdaughter of Isaac Penington. Their marriage was a happy one, marred only by the death of their first three children in infancy. Guli died in 1694, and two years later Penn married Hannah Callowhill and with her had seven children. Springett, the oldest surviving son of Penn's first marriage, was the most promising boy and the one closest to his father. Unfortunately, he died at nineteen, and none of the other boys proved strong enough characters to follow in their father's footsteps.

Penn's ability to maintain a relationship with the court, and even a close friendship with James II, while remaining true to his Quaker convictions has been the subject of some speculation. Did he make compromises in order to keep a foot in both worlds? Perhaps one or two. But his popularity seems to have stemmed from a certain grace of manner, rather than dubious behavior. "I know of no religion," he once wrote, "that destroys courtesy, civility, and kindness."

Because of this relationship with the court, Penn was able to get many Quakers released from prison, among them George Fox. But more important even than this, it permitted him to petition Charles II to grant him a colony in the new land across the sea. Charles had owed Penn's father, Sir William, sixteen thousand pounds. Instead of money, Penn suggested, let the King give him a tract of land in America north of Maryland, south of New York, and west of New Jersey.

After some delays, the King agreed. Charles II very probably was not too bothered by the debt to Sir William, but he liked young Penn and was glad to do him a favor under the guise of discharging a debt. Rather than calling the new colony, New Wales Sylvania, as Penn had requested, the King further showed his favor by naming it Pennsylvania. On March 4, 1681, the charter was signed, and shortly thereafter the King issued a declaration requiring all the people now living in the province to yield obedience to Penn. Next August the Duke of York added the three counties of Delaware to the royal grant. Unfortunately, the boundaries had never been properly established. It later developed that the land given to Maryland and Pennsylvania overlapped to such an extent that Baltimore was in Pennsylvania and Philadelphia in Maryland! But for the moment all seemed in order.

With a characteristic burst of energy, Penn threw himself into getting his new colony in shape. First he wrote to the present settlers, the three thousand Dutch, Swedes, and English already living in the area, promising them a just government. Then he began the job of recruiting settlers with a pamphlet entitled "Some Account of the Province of Pennsylvania in America." The capital city had to be planned. After consideration he named it Philadelphia, City of Brotherly Love, and laid it out as a gridiron with regularly spaced parks that it might always be "a greene countrie towne." William Markham, his cousin, was sent out before him with a letter of friendship for the Indians, and instructions to buy land from the Indians for the Penn family along the Delaware River, the future site of Pennsbury Manor, Penn's own residence. A trading company at this time offered him six thousand pounds for a monopoly of trade with the Indians, but this he refused, saying he would not "defile what came to me clean."

Most of all, however, Penn devoted himself to writing and

rewriting a Frame of Government. With the help of his friends John Locke and Algernon Sidney, he struggled to produce a document that would provide the new colony with a constitution embodying all his best thinking, and preserving the people from the meddling of future petty tyrants. He even preserved them against himself. "I propose that which is extraordinary, to leave myself and successors no power of doing mischief, that the will of one man may not hinder the good of the whole country."

Penn felt it was his duty to establish the best possible form of government for his new colony.

> The nations [he wrote] want a precedent—and because I have been somewhat exercised about the nature and end of government among men, it is reasonable to expect that I should endeavor to establish a just and righteous one in this province that others may take example by it . . . there may be room there, though not here, for such a holy experiment.

The effort to build such a community in the world, rather than to retreat from the world, he regarded as a Christian duty. "True Godliness don't turn men out of the world, but enables them to live better in it, and excites their endeavors to mend it."

A Whig, Penn was an early enthusiast for the rule of the people. His ideas, set out in the preface of his Frame of Government, make clear his belief in the people.

> Government seems to me a part of religion itself, a thing sacred in its institution and end . . . and government is free to the people under it, whatever be the frame, where the laws rule and the people are party to these laws. . . . Wherefore governments rather depend upon men than men upon governments. Let men be good, and the government cannot be bad. If it be ill, they will cure it. But if men be bad, let the government be never so good, they will endeavor to warp and spoil it to their turn.

A colony made up of Quakers, Penn believed, therefore could not be other than good. In fact, though there were safeguards built into the constitution, Penn seems to have thought that there would be very little need of the coercive aspects of the state, which would finally wither away, leaving a holy community.

To Penn's original Frame of Government were added fifteen fundamental laws passed by the first sessions of the Pennsylvania Assembly. From 1683 to 1701 there were several major revisions in the document, but from 1701 to 1776 the constitution of Pennsylvania remained unaltered. When the founding fathers met in Philadelphia to draw up a constitution for the United States, the Pennsylvania charter—still containing portions of Penn's original work—served as a model in many respects.

Basically the Frame of Government as amended established religious liberty, provided for a council and an assembly elected by the people to make the laws, called for trial by jury, and initiated a liberal penal system. Only two offenses, murder and treason, were to merit the death sentence.

With everything at last in order, Penn set sail for his new colony aboard the ship *Welcome.* He landed in New Castle late in October, 1682, and pushed on to the present site of the city of Philadelphia where he established his headquarters. Here he spent almost two years, getting this new colony in working order, becoming acquainted with the Indians, and supervising the construction of his new home, Pennsbury Manor, on the Delaware. He loved this spot, with its sweeping view across the river, and looked forward to installing his beloved Guli in the manor house and settling down for a lifetime in the New World.

Unhappily, it was not to be. His wife fell ill and was forced month by month to put off the trip across the ocean. Meanwhile Penn himself found it necessary to return to England to dispute

Lord Baltimore, who was pressing his claim at court for much of Penn's land. In 1684, Penn left the new colony for an absence which he expected to be brief but which stretched out for fifteen long years. From 1699 to 1701 he was back for a two-year visit; otherwise he governed his Holy Experiment from a London desk.

Politically that experiment was not an unqualified success. Like new nations anywhere in the world the colonies of America had many growing pains. Pennsylvania, despite its charter, was no exception. The new settlers were too busy establishing themselves and their families to have much time to spend in the novel pursuit of self-government. Neither the legislative bodies nor the courts met regularly. As a result, problems of lawlessness arose. There was constant bickering between the Council and the Assembly, between the Pennsylvania counties and the lower counties comprising modern Delaware, between the developing merchant class in the city and the farmers in the country. Feuds developed between the leaders of these various groups. "Be not so governmentish," Penn once wrote in exasperation.

Penn had other reasons to be exasperated. Since acquiring Pennsylvania he had spent a great deal of money on the development of the new colony. In return he hoped for a reasonable income from the sale of lands and from quitrents (feudal dues of a shilling or a bushel of wheat for every hundred acres). But the new settlers were slow about paying for the land, and many were simply opposed to the very idea of quitrents. Penn, accustomed to living as a gentleman, had no source of income except from his land, especially after he lost his Irish holdings. In the years following the birth of the Holy Experiment he slid gradually deeper and deeper into personal debt.

To straighten matters out he sent various men as his

personal representatives. Some of these were poor choices and one, the Puritan John Blackwell, a disaster. Penn was no judge of men. At home he trusted his affairs to an agent, Philip Ford, who regularly cheated him, egged on by a greedy wife. Several times Penn signed papers which the Fords prepared for his signature without reading them through. In one of these papers he discovered later, to his horror, he had actually conveyed Pennsylvania to the Fords, and had been renting it back from them since then.

From the point of view of the English crown, Pennsylvania was far from a satisfactory colony. The Quaker settlers regularly refused to vote sums of money to the common defense of the colonies, since this violated their pacifist views and since they felt themselves to have nothing to fear from the Indians. In addition, the new colonists were a poor source of revenue for the mother country. The British Board of Trade suspected that the Pennsylvanians winked at a certain amount of smuggling, and perhaps a little outright piracy, rather than see American gold on its way to British coffers. In an effort to tighten up its control of trade, the crown established admiralty courts which functioned with no regard whatsoever to Pennsylvania's own civil courts. Disagreements escalated.

In 1694, Penn was out of favor for his friendship with the deposed James II. The British crown, seizing the opportunity, took Penn's colony away from him and placed it under Governor Fletcher of New York with orders that he raise defense revenue from the prosperous Pennsylvanians. At first the colonists refused, but finally they were forced to compromise, giving a sum "to feed the Hungrie and Cloath the Naked." United by their common opposition to Fletcher, they were delighted when the colony was restored to Penn two years later, and more ready thereafter to cooperate with his agents.

Personal tragedy stalked Penn throughout the early years of
the Holy Experiment. His beloved Guli died in 1694, and
though he married again, and produced a new family of children,
he never quite recovered from the loss of his first love. His
financial affairs were an endless source of worry. In 1708 he
was declared bankrupt, the Fords coming forward with the
claim that he owed them fourteen thousand pounds. British
Friends, learning for the first time of his financial plight, in-
vestigated, persuaded the Fords to reduce their claim to seven
thousand, raised the money, and arranged for Penn to be released from Old Bailey. The long years of strain, however, had
taken their toll, and in 1712 he suffered a stroke and a loss of
memory. Though he lived on until 1718, he was never again
able to take a hand in shaping Pennsylvania.

William Penn was in many ways a man ahead of his time.
In addition to his Holy Experiment, he devised a plan for the
federation of the American colonies. In 1693 he brought forth
a blueprint for world government, or a federation of the states
of Europe. Though the Holy Experiment itself did not result
in the calm and harmonious government of which he had
dreamed, it possibly had no more, and probably less, conflict
than other new experiments in democracy. The fact that the
experiment was made permitted the framers of the United
States Constitution to draw upon the trials and errors of
Pennsylvania's one hundred years of history. By 1786 it had
been demonstrated that Penn's basic concept of putting the
power in the people could be made to work as a valid basis
of government.

In one respect at least Penn was entirely successful. From
the time of his first arrival in Pennsylvania until his death, he
maintained excellent relations with the Indians. A cornerstone
of his policy was to buy the land, even paying twice if two

Friends Meeting House and Academy, Fourth and Chestnut streets, Philadelphia, in 1789. (*Courtesy the Quaker Collection, Haverford College Library. Photo by Norman Wilson.*)

Penn's treaty with the Indians. (*Painting by Benjamin West. Courtesy the Pennsylvania Academy of the Fine Arts.*)

tribes held disputing claims, and to honor these boundaries with scrupulous care.

According to legend, Penn met with the Indians at Shackamaxon in November, 1682, to make his great treaty for Pennsylvania, "the only treaty," according to Voltaire, "never sworn to and never broken." There is no evidence that this particular treaty occurred, though it is very probable that some treaty was made in Shackamaxon that fall. Penn, however, never bought all of his new colony at one time. He purchased strips up the Delaware, measured from the mouth of one creek to the mouth of the next, as need increased.

In addition to his land policy, Penn won the sympathies of the Indians by his general attitude of respect toward them. Within a short period of time he had learned enough of their language to converse without a translator, and whenever opportunity arose he threw himself into their games of skill. They called him *Onas,* the Indian word for Quill (as near as they could come to "pen"). For many years the Quakers were called by the Indians the sons of Onas, and therefore their friends.

As a settlement, Pennsylvania was successful from the beginning. Penn's liberal policy of accepting immigrants regardless of creed and nationality brought shiploads of new colonists from Holland, Germany, and France, as well as the British Isles. Philadelphia grew rapidly. Neat frame houses sprang up along the well-planned streets while more settlers, awaiting the construction of their houses, lived in caves cut into the high river banks. New industries burst into being as shipload after shipload of industrious artisans, representing almost every known trade of the day, arrived.

Set on the wide Delaware, the port of Philadelphia bustled with activity, as ships arrived from London laden with supplies for the new settlers and ships departed laden with fur, lumber, flour, and pork. London could not use these products, so the Pennsylvanians early began to trade at intermediate points, such as Lisbon or the West Indies, where they could sell their cargoes and buy such products as sugar, molasses, rum, or wine, all in demand in England. A thriving triangular trade developed, permitting the colonists to obtain the currency they needed to buy products for their new enterprises.

Soon Philadelphia had outstripped Boston and New York to become the unchallenged commercial leader of the New World. In the tranquil and prosperous years of the eighteenth century, large fortunes began to accumulate in the hands of Philadelphia's Quaker merchants. The majority of the settlers had been drawn from the artisan or yeoman class in England, and had arrived in the new country penniless, if not in debt for the voyage, but within a few decades a Quaker aristocracy, based on wealth and status, began to emerge.

Quakers believed in thrift and industry as values in themselves. There was to be, according to George Fox, no separation between the sacred and the profane; every act should be sacramental just as every day of the week was to be regarded as equally dedicated to God. Penn urged his settlers to practice diligence and frugality and told them, "A Penny Saved Is a Penny Got," sixty years before Benjamin Franklin published *Poor Richard's Almanac.*

The thrifty and diligent Quakers of Philadelphia probably did not set out to become wealthy, but their industrious habits, their modest personal expenses, and the wealth of the new country all helped to make them so. The sons and daughters of well-to-do Quakers married, and family dynasties were established. Often the same Quaker merchants met as overseers of the meeting, as members of Council, and as business partners. The affairs of the new colony, of the Society of Friends, and of the countinghouses became intertwined.

Though the Quaker testimony against extravagances of dress and mode of living still held sway over their consciences, the wealthy Quakers slowly increased their standard of living. They built handsome city houses along the streets of Philadelphia, and often owned country houses, or "plantations" as well, sometimes as far out in the country as half way to Germantown. They entertained visitors at rich banquets, kept wine cellars, and wore the best, if the most sober, goods. A few even had coaches, pulled by four matched horses and attended by servants in livery.

These well-to-do Quakers did not allow themselves to spend money on such idle amusements as gambling, dancing, art, music, or the theater. They did, however, indulge their interest in books and reading. Several built large libraries covering every aspect of the literature of the day. Many were interested in science as a hobby and a recreation. The Quaker inductive approach to religion nourished an inductive approach to education and observation, and helped to produce a scientific spirit. By the middle of the eighteenth century Philadelphia was enjoying a flowering of scientific endeavor in which several Quakers played an active role. Institutions such as the American Philosophical Society and Pennsylvania Hospital were founded with considerable support from the wealthy Quakers.

One of these was James Logan, the Scottish clerk whom William Penn had brought to Philadelphia in 1699. Logan was a faithful servant to Penn and his family, in private affairs and later in the government of the colony. At first he was kept poor trying to meet the proprietor's expenses from his own pocket, but after a while he developed his own interests in the fur trade. As he grew comfortable he invested in books, until his library became one of the finest in colonial America. At Stenton, the country house he built north of the city, he pursued scientific studies. His work on the cross-fertilization of corn made an important contribution to the botanical studies of the time.

In public life Logan was a controversial figure. His loyalty to Penn and the Penn family made him a defender of the aristocratic rather than the democratic principle in Pennsylvania politics. Though a nominal Quaker he was never in very good standing, thanks in part to the fact that he favored defensive war. On the other hand, his policy toward the Indians was excellent, and helped preserve the Quaker peace. Whatever the complexities of statecraft, he liked to retire to the sanctuary of his library and his laboratory and to the quiet pursuits of pure reason. At his death his large library was left to the people of Philadelphia.

With the help of men like Logan, Philadelphia might in fact have become the intellectual as well as the commercial capital of the New World during this period had it not been for the continued Quaker prejudice against higher education. In Philadelphia, as elsewhere, the Quakers established small elementary schools for their own children and took in poor scholars free of charge. In several places this latter policy led to the creation of the first public schools. But the Friends remembered their old feelings against Oxford and Cambridge as the sites of the training of hireling ministers, and saw no need in Philadelphia for an institution such as Boston's Harvard College. A few Quakers were active in founding the Academy which later became the College of Philadelphia, but they lost interest when the Anglicans took over the Academy and began to turn it into an institution of higher education.

Nevertheless, the scions of the wealthiest Quaker families were taught Greek and Latin, and quite a few were sent to the Continent for a grand tour before taking their places beside their fathers in the countinghouses. Not surprisingly, several came back from Europe ready to renounce their Quaker background altogether. A group of fashionable Quakers, or "wet" Quakers, developed. Most of them were Quaker in name only, and many joined the Anglican Church. The conversion of wealthy Quakers to the Episcopal Church still occurs in Philadelphia's Main Line and Chestnut Hill sections today. "A carriage and pair does not long continue to drive to a meetinghouse," the Quakers say.

Even among those Quakers who remained faithful, the development of prosperity had an adverse effect upon their spiritual lives. The wellsprings of Quaker inspiration seemed to be drying up; the meetings becoming formal. Visitors from England, as well as native reformers such as Job Scott and John Woolman, began to express concern. Wrote Samuel Fothergill in 1756:

> Their fathers came into the country and bought large tracts of land for a trifle; their sons found large estates come into their possession, and a profession of religion which was partly national, which descended like a patrimony from their fathers, and cost as little. They settled in ease and affluence, and whilst they made the barren wilderness a fruitful field, suffered the plantation of God to be as a field uncultivated, and a desert. . . . A people who had thus beat their swords into plowshares with the bent of their spirits to this world, could not instruct their offspring in the statutes they had themselves forgotten.

The picture, however, is not one of black and white. It was during this very period of affluence that Philadelphia Quakers began the development of the social concerns which have been among the lasting contributions of the Society to the life of the United States. The Friends Alms House on Walnut Street was open to all "without distinction of sects or parties," and Friends pressed the corporation of Philadelphia to build the first public almshouse. Quakers in England had been the first in the world to recognize that the mentally ill deserved gentle care, rather than punishment. Pennsylvania Hospital, which the Quakers helped found, was the first institution in the New World to pro-

vide medical and occupational care for the insane. Early Quaker
concern for prisons and prison reform led to the creation of the
Philadelphia Society for Alleviating the Miseries of Public
Prisons.

It was during this period, too, that the Quakers in government
became strong advocates of the democratic principle. During
Logan's period of active participation there had been a split between a conservative and a liberal wing, but after his retirement
in 1727 the Friends united in common opposition to a new
conservative group, dominated by Anglicans and loyal to the
crown. Eventually the Quakers themselves withdrew from government but the "Quaker Party," under the leadership of Benjamin Franklin, continued to represent liberty-loving elements in
the Pennsylvania population—the Quakers, the Germans, and
the Mennonites—up to the Revolutionary War.

Throughout this time the Quakers of Philadelphia developed
a deepening concern for the Indians. Experience regularly confirmed their faith that loving kindness toward the peoples of the
American forests would be met by loving kindness. What was
more, this policy was proving to be a good business. The long
period of peace with the Indians which Pennsylvania enjoyed
probably contributed more than any other single factor to the
material success of the new colony.

In Pennsylvania as elsewhere the Quaker success with the Indians seemed to spring from a predisposition to think well of them.
In 1688 a rumor reached Philadelphia from two apparently independent sources that five hundred warriors were about to attack
the settlement. Caleb Pusey, a member of Council, and five other
unarmed Friends went out into the woods to the site of the al-
leged rendezvous of the war party. Here they found the Indian
chief who was supposedly leading the attack, lying in bed surrounded by his women and children. When told of the rumor

he explained that he had some claims for unpaid debts, but was far from ready to go on the warpath. "The authors of the report should be burned to death," he declared.

The Quakers soon observed the bad effects of rum upon the Indians and advised their members against selling any strong liquor to them. ". . . it is not consistent with the honor of Truth, for any that makes a profession thereof, to sell Rum or other strong liquors to the Indians, because they use them not to moderation, but to Excess and Drunkenness," a 1685 minute states.

As long as the Quakers were in control of the colony, the policy of paying the Indians a fair price for land was maintained. Where other settlers were sometimes guilty of befuddling the Indians with liquor and then driving a sharp bargain, the Quakers were particularly scrupulous to keep liquor away from the bargaining table.

Sadly enough it was William Penn's own children who created the first serious breach in this land policy. None of Penn's sons was ever more than a nominal Quaker, and all of them were eager to extract what financial gain they could from their father's Pennsylvania holdings.

In 1686 Penn had agreed with local Indian chiefs to buy land in Bucks County as far as a man could walk in a day and a half. Both Penn and the Indians understood this to mean about thirty miles. Thomas Penn, however, desired land above the thirty-mile point, and had even encouraged squatters to settle there. The Minisink Tribe of the Delaware, who held the land, refused to sell it, and in desperation young Penn turned to artifice. In 1737 two athletes were especially trained to make the "walk" at record clip. To aid them further, underbrush was cut away, horses provided to carry supplies and boats to ferry them across streams. As a result the "walk" was stretched to cover sixty miles instead of thirty. The surveyors increased the fraud by slanting the upper boundaries far to the north to include all the desired territory. The Walking Purchase has ever since been remembered by the Indians as a synonym of infamy.

Conscious that they had been cheated, the Minisink did not move, and the Quaker-dominated legislature refused to appropriate funds to force them to do so. Thus matters stood until 1742, when the anti-Quaker forces held a convention with the Iroquois, then overlords of the Delawares, and after a good bit of liquor and feasting, persuaded the ruling tribes to censure the Minisink for their refusal to obey the terms of the Walking Purchase.

This marked the end of the Quaker Peace policy. Though the Minisink moved west in obedience to their overlords, they were sullen and hostile, ready to take offense. The new settlers who had been pouring into Pennsylvania's western communities for the past two decades were primarily Scotch-Irish. They did not share the Quaker view of the Indian, and they were quick to respond to the slightest sign of Indian truculence or discontent. Grievances multiplied as the proprietors followed more and more the dubious policy of selling the land to settlers before it had been officially purchased from the Indians. Many of the newcomers in addition simply squatted.

In 1754 all these troubles came to a climax when the proprietors bought from the Iroquois practically all the remaining lands of western Pennsylvania. The French, at war with the English, now found the opportunity they had been looking for and promptly took advantage of it. By playing upon the grievances of the Indians they persuaded them to go on the warpath. After the defeat of General Braddock at Fort Duquesne, the Pennsylvania Indians at last gave vent to their rage and frustration, and the peace which had lasted over seventy years was broken.

The new Scotch-Irish frontiersmen were the first to be attacked. Their houses and barns were burned, their men killed and scalped, their women and children taken into slavery. Their appeals to Philadelphia for military help at first produced no results. In order to make their protest against this policy, they loaded several of their dead upon carts, took them to Philadelphia, and left them in front of the State House.

To this protest, as well as pressure from the home government, the Philadelphians at last yielded. In April, 1756, the governor of Pennsylvania declared war and offered a bounty for Indian scalps. The Quaker members of the Assembly were now faced with a delicate problem of conscience. If they remained in office they would be party to the waging of the war. On the other hand, if they left, they could no longer restrain their fellows in belligerence, or influence them to seek peace.

The problem was not a new one. For the past sixty years Quaker legislators had been dodging the issue by voting money "for the Queen's use" or "for the King's use" or "for the purchase of Bread, Beef, Pork, Flour, Wheat, and other Grain" when money for defense was demanded. This time however no subterfuge would serve. After a few weeks six Quaker members of the Assembly requested leave to resign their seats, stating that "the present situation of Public Affairs calls upon us for services in a military Way, which from a Conviction of Judgment, after mature Deliberation, we cannot comply with."

A contributing factor in persuading the Quakers to withdraw was a rumor then current that the Board of Trade, in response to a request from the anti-Quaker forces in Pennsylvania, was about to pass a law requiring an oath of all members of all colonial legislatures. This would have disqualified Friends not only in Pennsylvania but other colonies as well. Alarmed by this prospect, the Meeting for Sufferings in London sent two emissaries to persuade the Pennsylvania Quakers to withdraw from the Assembly. Before these two had a chance to arrive, however, the American Quakers had made their decision.

The withdrawal of the Quakers from the government of Pennsylvania marked a turning point in the history of the Society of Friends in America. Up to this point the Quakers had been willing to live in the world, and had tried to put their principles to work in the conduct of public affairs. As a result they found themselves engaged in a series of compromises both in the State House and the countinghouse. Leaders like the saintly young John Woolman of New Jersey were beginning to warn that the spiritual life of the Society was in grave danger. With withdrawal, the Quakers chose to turn their backs on the exercise of power, and to devote their energies to the development of a separate, holy community. This course, too, had its perils.

A continuing aspect of the dilemma of Quakers is the payment of war taxes. If Quakers will not fight, should they allow their dollars to do so? In 1755 the question of paying taxes for war purposes was debated in Philadelphia Yearly Meeting. Although there was no unanimity, twenty-one Friends signed an epistle stating that "as we cannot be concerned in wars and fightings, so neither ought we to contribute thereby by paying the tax directed by said act, though suffering be the consequence of our refusal."

This was not to be a negative gesture. In 1756, just after the outbreak of the war, the Quakers formed The Friendly Association for Gaining and Preserving Peace with the Indians by Pacific Measures, pledging to its support "a much larger part of our estate than the heaviest taxes of a war can be expected to require." In the next two years they spent some five thousand pounds arranging a series of conferences between Tedyuscung, chief of the Delawares, and the governor, and offering gifts to the disgruntled Indians. At the second of these conferences Tedyuscung refused to appear unless the Quakers were present as witnesses. Finally, at the third, the governor gave some recognition that the "walk" had been unfair (while not offering to give back the land) and peace was declared.

The border, however, remained uneasy, and resentment against the Quakers for "coddling" the Indians continued to grow among the new settlers. During the height of the war of 1756 the Quaker frontier families had remained untouched, a fact which made their neighbors deeply suspicious. In 1765 a group of frontier vigilantes, who called themselves the Paxton boys, decided to teach the Indians and the Quakers a lesson by killing off the remnant of the Conestoga tribe of Lancaster County, whom they accused of giving information to the other, more warlike Indians. About twenty Conestogas, mainly women and children, were murdered in their homes, or in the Lancaster jail, where they had been hastily placed for safety.

The Paxton boys next decided to march on Philadelphia where the Quakers had removed a band of Moravian Indians for safety. When two hundred of these frontiersmen camped in Germantown, Philadelphians arose in arms to defend the Indians. Many young Quakers forgot all about their scruples and took up rifles with the rest. The meetinghouse was used as a barracks, and the guns were stacked in the gallery.

Despite all this bellicosity, peaceful methods prevailed. Benjamin Franklin (sympathetic with the Friends but no pacifist) marched with a delegation of citizens to meet the Paxton boys, discussed their demands, and mollified them sufficiently to send them home without the scalps of the Moravians. The Quakers, however, felt it necessary to deal with their young men who had forgotten themselves so much as to take up arms. A few of these confessed error, but many more defended themselves, and some later took up arms in the Revolutionary War. But that is another story.

# 5

# The middle years of American Quakerism: 1775–1875

The American Revolution was a time of great testing for the Quakers. Throughout the colonial period Friends felt no sympathy for the wars in which their neighbors were occasionally engaged. They were wars of European origin, between Great Britain and Spain or Great Britain and France, having little real bearing on the lives of the American settlers. And they were wars in which the great powers involved the Indians by exploiting their sense of grievance and inflaming tribe against tribe. The Quakers were strongly against this misuse of the red man's loyalties.

The Revolution, however, was a different matter. The deep vein of democratic sentiment that threaded its way through Quaker belief had made the American Quakers liberty-loving from the start. By the middle of the eighteenth century the majority of them were objecting to Britain's increasing efforts to dominate and control colonial trade. In Pennsylvania the democratic Quaker party opposed the loyalist Proprietary party. Such Quakers as Stephen Hopkins in Rhode Island and John Dickinson of Pennsylvania took the lead in stating the position of the colonists in newspaper journals of the day.

Even the conservative Philadelphia merchants were active in the beginnings of the resistance movement. In 1765, some fifty of them, including the wealthy Pembertons and the Whartons, signed the nonimportation agreement to defeat the Stamp Act. In 1773, two Philadelphia Quaker firms, T & I Wharton, and James and Drinker, turned back a shipment of tea from England. Typical of Quaker Philadelphia, the tea was neither dumped nor burned but carefully consigned back to London, and the captain of the ship given money to cover his return passage.

By 1775, however, the revolutionary fervor of their compatriots was too fiery for the Quakers. Sympathetic as they were, they had a testimony, they felt, not only against war but against revolution itself. They remembered the words of George Fox in 1685:

> Whatever bustlings or troubles or tumults or outrages should rise in the world keep out of them, but keep in the Lord's power and in the peaceable truth that is over all, in which power you seek the peace and good of all men, and live in the love which God has shed abroad in your hearts through Jesus Christ, in which love nothing is able to separate you from God and Christ.

From their earliest days, Quakers had believed that they must be obedient to the government, whenever their conscience did not force them to oppose it. In 1775, they saw the government to be the King's. Much as they had opposed the rule of England over the colonists in the past, they now felt they must acknowledge the throne as the legitimate government. It was their duty, therefore, they believed, not only to maintain a policy of strict Quaker neutrality in the fighting, but also to refuse to cooperate with the Continental Congress. Friends not only refused to be drafted into the militia and to pay war taxes, but they also would not use the money which the new American government had begun to produce.

This somewhat tortured point of view led many of their fellow Americans to regard the Quakers as Tories or British sympathizers. In actual fact the majority favored the American cause, though they felt they could not show this by word or deed. Most of the New England Quakers, southern Quakers, and country Quakers sided with the colonists, while the stronghold of British sentiment was in Philadelphia and New York. Only six Quakers were disowned for joining the British forces, while between four and five hundred Friends were expelled from their meetings for participation in the American cause.

Of these, only a small number actually fought. Members were disowned for paying war taxes to the American patriots, for paying fines in lieu of military service, or paying fines for their refusal to collect military taxes. One of the first to leave the Society was Thomas Mifflin, later to become a Revolutionary general and a governor of the state of Pennsylvania. Among those that followed was Betsy Ross, the seamstress who is supposed to have designed the American flag; Nathanael Greene, a great Revolutionary War general, was originally a Rhode Island Quaker.

Although disowned by their meetings, many of these "fighting Quakers" did not feel comfortable in other churches. They were still Quakers, they felt, disagreeing with their coreligionists only over the question of participation in the war. In Philadelphia they founded a small group called the Free Quakers, and built a meetinghouse that is still standing at Fifth and Arch Streets. Their numbers, small at first, dwindled over the years, and the group finally died out altogether about 1820.

In 1777, just before the British occupied Philadelphia, City Council arrested forty prominent citizens as British sympathizers, and asked them to swear an oath of allegiance to the new government. Among these were a number of prominent Quakers, including Israel Pemberton, sometimes called "king of the Quakers." Ultimately twenty Philadelphians, including seventeen Quakers, who refused to swear this oath were banished for a time to Winchester, Virginia. They were not particularly ill treated, but they were unprepared for the journey in the dead of winter, and two elderly Quakers died as a result.

Throughout their banishment the group wrote vigorous protests against the summary procedures taken against them, which violated not only their civil liberties but set a bad precedent for the new nation. Finally, a deputation of wives and mothers of the prisoners went to see General Washington, and were able to convince him that the charges against the prisoners were false. With a half-apology from the Council, the group was allowed to return.

When the American troops regained Philadelphia after the British occupation, anti-Quaker sentiment was very strong. The homes of many of the Quakers were stoned, and some individuals were hooted through the streets. An oath of allegiance was demanded of all school teachers, and a number of Quakers who refused to swear lost their jobs.

Elsewhere also the Quakers suffered for their pacifism. Nantucket Island was a stronghold of Quakerdom, and therefore suspected by the American patriots as a stronghold of Tory sentiment. As a result the islanders came close to starvation. The citizens of Massachusetts cut off their provisions, while the British captured their whalers. Only by shooting game and seafowl were the inhabitants of Nantucket able to stay alive.

One Nantucket Quaker, William Rotch, could have grown rich on the war. As the leading shipowner of the island he was involved in many financial transactions. Just before the war he was given a large supply of muskets and bayonets in payment for a debt. With the outbreak of hostilities both the British and the American armies attempted to requisition them. Instead, he sold some to his islanders for fowling pieces and got rid of the rest.

"As this instrument is purposely made and used for the destruction of mankind and I cannot put into one man's hands to destroy another that which I cannot use myself in the same way, I refuse to comply with thy demand," he told an American officer. "I would gladly have beaten them into pruning hooks. As it was, I took an early opportunity of throwing them into the sea."

In New Jersey and the southern colonies, the Quakers suffered heavy property losses for their refusal to pay taxes. Their homes, barns, and meetinghouses were commandeered, their horses and cattle taken. Many were imprisoned. In Virginia, fourteen Quakers were drafted into the militia and punished severely when they refused to handle their rifles.

Despite these troubles of their own, the Quakers were moved by the plight of their fellow citizens during the Revolutionary War. In the winter of 1775–1776, when the city of Boston was under siege, the Friends in Pennsylvania and elsewhere raised a large sum of money and turned it over to the New England Meeting for Sufferings to use in the relief of citizens of Boston. Though neither the British nor the American forces would allow the Quakers to pass through the lines, the generals permitted some of the funds to be sent to Boston Quakers for distribution to the suffering in the city "without distinction to sects or parties." Moses Brown of Rhode Island led a committee which rode on horseback through the dead of winter distributing the rest to the poor in adjacent towns. Among those aided was Salem, which publicly thanked the Quakers, noting that one hundred years previously the Quakers had been whipped through its streets.

In New York, Friends refused to give the Committee of Safety a listing of all male Quakers, and later, when General Tryon occupied the city, also refused to provide stockings and other comforts for the British troops. Several Friends meanwhile served in the meetinghouse, which had been turned into a hospital. Elsewhere other meetinghouses were used for this purpose and other Friends nursed the wounded. The long tradition of Quaker neutrality and war relief was now begun.

Throughout the war years the Quakers continued to suffer for their efforts to remain neutral. When the American forces were victorious and the new nation independent, many could not help being secretly pleased. In 1789 the Quakers acknowledged their reconciliation with the new American government by congratulating Washington on his election as President. At the same time they reaffirmed their belief that they "can take no part in any warlike measures on any occasion or under any power." Washington replied that in his opinion liberty of conscience was a right, not a privilege:

> Your principles and conducts are well known to me, and it is doing the people called Quakers no more than justice to say that (except their declining to share with others in the burdens of common defence) there is no denomination among us who are more exemplary and useful citizens. I assure you very especially that in my opinion the conscientious scruples of all men should be treated with great delicacy and tenderness; and it is my wish and desire that the laws may always be

extensively accommodated to them as a due regard to the protection and essential interest of the nation may justify.

The Revolutionary War had a profound effect upon the Quakers, particularly the thirty thousand who lived in and around Philadelphia. Until 1775 the Friends had regarded their withdrawal from public life in 1756 as a temporary expedient. Indeed, it was hard to stay withdrawn. Devoted constituents, including the many German Mennonites and Brethren who had poured into Pennsylvania during the first half of the eighteenth century, kept voting Quakers into the Assembly whether they had stated they wanted to stand or not. Now, with the sudden unpopularity of the Friends, all this was changed. Rebuffed, the Quakers felt they had no future in public life. Instead, they turned to the task of purifying themselves as a peculiar people, and reforming their own separate society.

The processes of reformation, begun at an earlier period, were now intensified. Friends began to be more insistent that their children not mix with non-Friends at school, but have a guarded education. The evils of keeping a public house or drinking to excess were raised more frequently and more sternly with wayward members. A serious effort was made to return all members to a primitive simplicity in dress, habits, and furniture. Most important of all, members were now strenuously urged to rid themselves of slave-owning.

Stirred by the eloquent antislavery testimony of such men as John Woolman and Anthony Benezet, the various yearly meetings had been urging Friends to free their slaves from 1758 onward. In 1773, New England Yearly Meeting directed that those who persisted in owning slaves should be disowned. In 1776, Philadelphia, New York, and North Carolina took similar action. Baltimore followed in 1778 and Virginia in 1784.

For southern Friends the freeing of their slaves resulted in genuine hardships. Not only were the Quakers treated with hostility by their slave-owning neighbors, their freed slaves were also quickly seized and sold again. Often the Quakers had to start expensive lawsuits to try to prevent this. Sometimes the meetings themselves bought the slaves and looked for some area in the world where they might be safely freed. Meanwhile, in the economy of the South of that day, the Quakers who voluntarily freed their slaves reduced themselves and their families to virtual poverty.

Nevertheless, the Friends in the southern states were not slow to follow their northern brothers in putting the antislavery testimony into practice. Reluctant Friends had the aid of a gentle persuasion from such traveling Quaker ministers as Sarah Harrison, a remarkable Pennsylvanian who traveled through miles of wilderness in order to labor with Quaker slaveholders. Though an uneducated woman, Sarah was such an effective minister that at a single meeting she once persuaded slaveholders to manumit fifty slaves.

In 1787, just as the southern Friends were experiencing the worst troubles as a result of their abolitionist activities, the Northwest Territory, comprising the present states of Ohio, Indiana, Michigan, Illinois, Wisconsin, and Minnesota, was opened as free territory from which slavery was forever excluded. To many of the Quakers, it seemed as though their prayers had been answered. "I see the seed of God sown in abundance, extending far northward," Joseph Dew, a Quaker minister, announced to Trent River Monthly Meeting in North Carolina in 1799.

So began the first wave of the great westward migration of the Quakers, a movement which was to have a great effect upon the Society of Friends and upon the young nation of which they were a part. In the first decades of the nineteenth century, more

Quakers moved west than had come originally to the colonies from the home country. Throughout the century the tide rolled on until it reached the West Coast in the 1890's. Everywhere, the Quaker pioneers brought ideas of democracy, religious liberty, and racial equality to the frontier. But the frontier changed them too, producing changes in subsequent Quaker history.

From the South, whole meetings migrated to Ohio en masse, leaving the original parent body feeble or dead. This was the case with the Trent River Meeting, the Bush River Meeting, and a settlement of Friends in Wrightsborough, Georgia. From other meetings, groups of families departed together. At first the home meetings tried to hold back the tide. The appeal of the new territories, rich, fertile, and free, was, however, too strong. By 1820, it has been estimated there were twenty thousand Friends west of the Alleghenies, and new meetings had been established throughout Ohio and Indiana.

The trip west was long and arduous. In 1805, it took the Wright family of Baltimore two months of rugged wagon travel to reach Ohio. The twelve-year-old daughter, Rachel, who kept a diary, described going over Laurel Hill in the Alleghenies: "The wagons would seem to pitch from rock to rock and the descent was so steep that should we pitch over it would be hard telling where to land." Members of her family became sick, the food supply was low, and often they slept out under the stars. When they finally reached Ohio, the family of fourteen had to share a one-room log cabin set in the midst of a dark forest. Sometimes a brother would go off in search of game and be lost for a time. His return was a time of great rejoicing. "Persons who have never lived in the wilderness can have but little conception of our feelings on these occasions."

Westward the wave continued to crest and break. By 1838, a monthly meeting had been established in Salem, Iowa, and a preparative meeting in Kansas in 1858. At the end of the century Quakers were among the pioneers that pressed on to the West Coast. A chart of their progress can be made from the dates of the establishment of the yearly meetings: Ohio in 1813, Indiana in 1821, Western (western Indiana) in 1858; Iowa in 1863; Canada in 1867; Kansas in 1872; Wilmington (Ohio) in 1892; Oregon in 1893; California in 1895; and Nebraska in 1908.

Though the main current of the western migration poured through Ohio, lesser tributaries followed parallel courses to the north and south. Even before the move from North Carolina to Ohio began, a number of Friends crossed the Blue Ridge Mountains into Tennessee. At about the same time a movement got underway taking Quakers from the New England and eastern New York meetings into western New York, Canada, and Michigan.

Life on the frontier was hard for Quaker and non-Quaker alike. The forests had to be cleared, log cabins built, food and clothing for the family made from the products of the farm. Settlements were far apart, and a journey to visit neighboring Friends a difficult undertaking. Against great odds the Quakers established schools for their children and meetinghouses for themselves. But the education was rudimentary, and the spiritual life within the meetinghouses at low ebb.

Across the mountains and through the virgin forests the itinerant Public Friends of the nineteenth century came from England and from the eastern states to oversee the spiritual welfare of these pioneering Friends. Unhappily, the reports they made of conditions among the pioneering Friends were often negative. Morals everywhere on the frontier were low, and the migrating Quakers were not immune. Disownments for excessive drinking, for fighting, for adultery, for fornication, and for the use of bad language appear in the minutes of early meetings along with the more usual complaints of marrying out, taking arms, or dancing to a fiddler. Though the overseers sought to protect the good name of the Society of Friends by dealing strictly with these wrongdoers, many visiting Friends felt there was too much emphasis on the letter of the law, and too little attention paid to the nourishment of the spiritual life of the settlers.

If the frontier meetings lacked an abundant spiritual life, the fault did not lie wholly with frontier conditions. Throughout the East as well, Quakerism was in a decline during the first three decades of the nineteenth century. Visiting British ministers found the youth "raw," the meetings "dull and unspiritual," and discipline strongly enforced and yet curiously ineffective. These were the conditions which precipitated the great crisis of separation in the history of American Quakerism.

Many forces were at work to create these conditions. Throughout the eighteenth century the discipline within the Society of Friends was slowly tightened. In the early days, anyone could belong to the Children of the Light who had a direct religious experience. There were no formal rules for membership. By the 1730's, however, the Society felt some need to obtain a list of members' children, so that each meeting might know for whom they were responsible, both morally, and—in case of need—financially. Asking that adult Friends provide lists of their children, the Society inadvertently created the practice of recognizing "birthright" membership. From that day to this, children born of Quaker parents may automatically become birthright members. While new members are admitted to the meeting after writing a letter of application, and being visited by a committee which examines them to be sure they are clear in their own minds that they want to join Friends, birthright members need make no such profession of unity. Since the birthright do not necessarily share in the spiritual adventures of their parents, they have constituted, some feel, a deadweight on the Society.

As the practices of the Society of Friends became more codified, Books of Discipline were created by each yearly meeting. For many years these were kept by the clerk of the meeting in manuscript form, but toward the end of the eighteenth century they were printed. These books contain the "Advices" under which the ministers and elders performed their duties, and the "Queries," questions which the monthly meeting asked themselves on a regular basis. The queries were first used as a form of gathering information about the Society, but gradually became a form of self-examination. At first the queries were answered in a formal and detailed manner by the overseers and all the members knew both the questions and answers by heart. In recent years, however, they have been used to stimulate discussion and self probing among members of the meeting.

Among the queries answered each year by members of the Philadelphia Yearly Meeting are the following:

Are love and unity maintained among you?

Do you manifest a forgiving spirit and a care for the reputation of others?

When differences arise are endeavors made to settle them speedily and in a spirit of meekness and love?

What are you doing as individuals or as a meeting to insure equal opportunities in social and economic life for those who suffer discrimination because of race, creed or social class? To understand and remove the causes of war and develop the conditions and institutions of peace?

The development of distinct officers within the Society slowly emerged in the course of the eighteenth century. Ministers as such were never appointed in the Society of Friends. They manifested themselves to the meeting by revealing their gifts for the ministry, and were subsequently recognized. Gradually, however, the custom was developed of asking the various monthly meetings to record recognized ministers.

Elders were judicious and weighty Friends who were not necessarily gifted in the ministry, but whose job it was to watch over the spiritual life of the meeting, nurture the development of young ministers, and see that the messages given were doctrinally sound, Biblically correct, and in keeping with the customs of the Society. The elders generally sat on the facing bench (the first row of the seats forming the gallery), and kept a close watch for nodding members. If someone spoke too long or not in keeping with the spirit of the meeting, he was "eldered."

The process of eldering still goes on today. Sometimes a man or a woman suffers from a compulsion to speak in meeting. The things he has to say do not fit in with the general sense of the meeting which each worshiper is experiencing in private. His words go on and on, and shatter the peace of the meeting. In such circumstances an elder may rise and say, "Friend, I believe we have received the weight of thy message." In extreme cases, where the person is clearly suffering from an emotional disturbance, sometimes an elder will put a hand on his shoulder and gently nudge him to sit down.

The overseers were chosen by each meeting to care for the membership, keeping a sharp eye out for those who departed from Quaker simplicity, or drank to excess, or seemed to be headed for marital difficulties of one kind or another. Since the meeting had no pastor, the pastoral duties of guarding the flock was handled by the overseers. The role of the overseer is not always negative. In modern Quakerdom he concentrates on making sure that those who need help, find it.

In periods of growth, creativity, and expansion within the Society of Friends, the ministry is the strongest element. In periods of stagnation and decline the overseers and the elders are in control. The withdrawal of Friends from public life at the end of the Revolutionary War resulted in a tightening of discipline and consequently a strengthening of the elders. Throughout the decades following the establishment of the United States, while democratic ideas grew more and more prevalent, the Society of Friends was becoming more rigid and stratified.

It was at this period that Friends were most distinctly set apart as a peculiar people. They kept themselves and their children from contact with "the world's people," wore the distinctive plain dress, used the plain speech, married their young and buried their dead with stark simplicity. Many were actually hostile to art, music, fiction, and drama. They did not celebrate Christmas, believing every day of the year should be the same to Christians. They attended meeting twice a week: once on First Day and once on Fifth Day, and what leisure they had from shop or farm was devoted to the affairs of the meeting. To the outside world they appeared pious, stiff, and set apart; honest as the day is long but quick to make a penny.

Inside the home, however, there was warmth and gaiety. Quarterly and yearly meetings were a time for great intervisitation and entertaining of relatives. At the home of Lucretia Mott, the Quaker abolitionist, there were often as many as forty adults —"and a side table of children"—to sit down for dinner during yearly meeting week. Quaker journals of the period refer nostalgically to the good fun and good food of these gatherings. Children were treated with great gentleness and included from the first in the life of the meeting. "When I was two years old I began to be taken to the Quaker meeting," wrote Elizabeth Buffum Chace, a New England Quaker.

Within the larger family of the Society of Friends, meanwhile, tensions continued to multiply. One factor contributing to an ultimate explosion was the growing distance and distrust between city Friends and country Friends. The city Friends had grown rich and worldly in the course of the eighteenth century. Their material weight and political power carried over into the conduct of meeting affairs. At yearly meeting, great attention was given to the words of the prominent city Friends, while the country Friends often felt themselves to be brushed aside.

The most important difference arising within the Society in America in this period of history, however, was one of doctrine. Though Quakerism in its pure form is essentially creedless, more a method than a set of beliefs, it has tended to be influenced by the dominant creeds of the day. The first Quakers, surrounded by Christian Puritanism, naturally expressed their experiences and insights in current terminology. Men and women in all periods of history have joined the Society, attracted by the emphasis on reality in religious experience, but they have brought with them the symbols and formulas of the Church, whether Methodist or Baptist or Episcopal, which they have left behind. Though this tendency has kept Quakerism an evolving, experimental form of religious expression, it has also opened the door to much controversy.

Throughout the eighteenth century, Quakerism was under the influence of Quietism, a form of mysticism that emphasizes that man, without God, is incapable of goodness. The Creature is nothing, God is everything. Quietism grew up on the continent of Europe, and began to have an influence on British and then American Quakerism after 1725. Under Quietism, Quakers began to regard any "creaturely" activity to be at variance with the Inner Light. They ought not, they believed, prepare themselves in any way in advance for the meeting for worship, or much else in life, nor make any decisions about vital matters without a direct leading from the Spirit. To let go, to be nothing, to be absolutely quiet, was the only way to be open and ready for the breath of God's guidance.

As a result of the influence of Quietism, the silent meetings of the Quakers became silent indeed. Sometimes months passed without a message being spoken, the worshipers being afraid that it might be the creature and not the Spirit which prompted them to speak. Public Friends, traveling great distances to visit isolated American meetings, often came and went without giving their message, since they, too, were concerned that they not be led by creaturely vanity into vain speaking. Even the regular reading of the Bible was discouraged as too much creaturely activity. Among extreme Quietists, education of any sort was regarded as vain. Without Bible reading, without religious education, with nothing but the silent meetings for worship to guide them, some young Quakers grew up in this period with only a very general and foggy idea of the basic Christian faith.

Toward the end of the eighteenth century, Quakerism was affected by another and very different religious approach. This was the evangelical movement which came to its first flowering with John Wesley, the founder of Methodism, and later resulted in the low church movement among Anglicans. The evangelical movement emphasized direct religious experience, but it also demanded that the individual accept Christ as his savior, and stressed the doctrine of Christ's atonement on the cross for the sins of the world. It held that the scriptures should be regarded as direct revelations of God, and therefore as final authority. The leaders of the evangelical movement were interested in promoting education and Bible study, and in confronting such social problems as alcoholism, prison abuse, and slavery. They therefore appealed strongly to some of the more progressive Quakers of the day, though aspects of their doctrine were wholly unacceptable to Quaker Quietists.

The city Friends, being more progressive and open to new ideas, were the first to be converted to the new evangelical spirit. In 1806, Philadelphia Yearly Meeting revised its discipline and introduced for the first time an article making it a cause for disownment to "deny the divinity of our Lord and Savior Jesus Christ, the immediate revelation of the Holy Spirit, or the authenticity of the Scriptures." A movement to unite all the yearly meetings was begun at the same time by the evangelically oriented Quakers. Both conservative Friends who wanted to preserve the old-time Quakerism in its pure form, and liberal Friends, who wanted more freedom of conscience, were alarmed by this drive to impose evangelical doctrines on the Society as a whole.

All these conflicting tendencies came into sharp focus around the figure of a Long Island farmer. Elias Hicks, of Jericho, New York, was a Quaker Quietist of the old school, a minister in his monthly meeting, a devoted husband and father to eleven children. Despite a limited education, he had a rational, probing mind, and as a young man developed a distaste for dogma and a devotion to the search for truth. He believed that the Inner Light should be the sole authority, and that therefore the scriptures, the historical facts about the life of Jesus, should be studied as a means for inner religious experience, not accepted as authoritative in and of themselves.

As he grew in the ministry, Elias Hicks traveled more and more. He spoke out increasingly against slavery and the use of its products. He preached to most of the meetings on Long Island, and he visited Quaker groups up and down the eastern seaboard. Walt Whitman, who as a boy of ten heard Hicks speak, describes him as a "tall straight figure, neither stout nor very thin, dressed in drab cloth, clean-shaven face, forehead of great expanse, large clear black eyes, long or middling long white hair."

Born in 1748, Elias Hicks was an old man before he became the center of controversy. Evangelical Friends began to complain

Elias Hicks. (*Courtesy the Quaker Collection, Haverford College Library. Photo by Norman Wilson.*)

Southwest view of the Westtown Boarding School, Chester County, Pennsylvania, established in 1794. (*Courtesy the Quaker Collection, Haverford College Library. Photo by Norman Wilson.*)

that he was doctrinally unsound, particularly in regard to the crucifixion. There were a few unpleasant incidents when he spoke in meetings in and around Philadelphia. Some complained that he was forward, sitting with the ministers and expressing his views whether or not the membership wanted to hear him. Then a British Friend, Thomas Shillitoe, influenced by the evangelical movement, began an effort to dispute him. The elders of Philadelphia Yearly Meeting attempted to deal with Hicks on questions of doctrine, but their manner of doing so seemed highhanded and arrogant to Hicks and his friends. Feeling that his right to freedom of expression was being challenged, many Friends came to his defense who did not particularly agree with his theology. The struggle deepened into a conflict between the principles of individual liberty of conscience versus the right of the meeting to control what its members believed. The delicate balance which George Fox had created some one hundred and seventy years earlier between the individual and the group seemed to be threatened at last.

The conflict came to a head at the Philadelphia Yearly Meeting of 1827. The Hicksites, who were in the majority, attempted to nominate one of their group, John Comly, as clerk. The clerk in office, Samuel Bettle, representing the orthodox group, stood his ground. After several days of deadlock the Hicksite group, under Comly, decided to make "a quiet retreat from the scene of confusion." Amid great anguish, the two Quaker groups separated.

The great separation, thus begun, ran like a widening fissure in the earth throughout Philadelphia Yearly Meeting. Quarterly, monthly, and preparative meetings divided into Hicksite and Orthodox branches. Quarrels over the ownership of meeting property could not be kept within the Society but ended up dishearteningly in public lawsuits.

Often families were divided, and bitter feelings resulted. In a letter to a sister, a Philadelphia Quakeress describes the tragedy poignantly:

> The other evening as Jonathan, James, William and I were sitting in the parlour in full confabulation, Uncle Josiah came in. We spent a comfortable evening on the whole and yet way seemed—as of latter day it has done—closed up; which sort of reserve always chills the intercourse between Friends (Hicksite) and Orthodox and gives the heartache where warm friendship once existed.

Within Philadelphia Yearly Meeting, the Hicksites had the numerical advantage. When the separation was over, and the membership recounted, it was discovered that there were approximately 18,500 Hicksites to 7,350 Orthodox. Almost all the country meetings had large Hicksite majorities. In Philadelphia itself, however, this trend was reversed, the majority remaining Orthodox. The Orthodox had the largest number of ministers and elders within its fold and retained the control of Westtown School, the Quaker boarding school established in 1799. Shortly after the separation they established Haverford College. Years later the Hicksites established Swarthmore College and George School.

Unhappily the separation did not stop with Philadelphia, but spread throughout the Society. New York Yearly Meeting split in the spring of 1828, the majority going with the Hicksites, and Baltimore followed suit in the fall, over four-fifths joining the new movement. The newly created Indiana Yearly Meeting remained predominantly Orthodox, though a small group of Hicksites withdrew.

The stormiest and most tragic separation occurred in the Ohio Yearly Meeting. Both Elias Hicks and Thomas Shillitoe attended, and the meeting split almost exactly in two, with much bitterness. At the final climactic meeting, members of the Orthodox group attempted to prevent the Hicksites from entering the building, but were pushed aside. In the midst of an undignified scramble in which both groups attempted to seat rival clerks, someone called out that the gallery was falling. There was a virtual stampede for the doors, windows were broken, and several persons injured.

The spectacle of Quakers, the great advocates of peace, fighting among themselves, was appalling to their sympathizers and delightful to their enemies. The Friends lost their confidence in themselves to speak to the world's people and the world's problems. The spirit of bitterness between alienated sections of each meeting continued.

In 1837 a prominent Quaker evangelical, Joseph John Gurney, came to the United States for a three-year visit. Gurney was the next to youngest child in a family of eleven children. Rich, gay, handsome, talented, the Gurneys of Earlham Hall were in high regard with Quakers of the day. Elizabeth Gurney Fry, Joseph's elder sister, became a famous crusader for prison reform. Joseph himself was well educated and acquainted with many of the great religious thinkers of the day. He was for a time strongly attracted to the Church of England, which several of his brothers and sisters joined, but eventually decided to take his place in the Society of Friends, as an advocate of the new, or evangelical doctrines. Though he was a prominent and successful banker, he gave much of the rest of his life to writing and speaking for the Society.

In the United States, Gurney's good looks, eloquence, and attractive personality won him many adherents. His was a triumphant tour of American Quakerism, for he won hearts and minds everywhere. He brought religious revival to many Quaker meetings which had been in a comatose condition, and reinstated an interest in education and in Bible study, both of which had waned considerably during the long years of Quietism.

Gurney's visit, however, also stirred up more controversy.

Within the Orthodox wing of the Society there remained a group of people who had regarded Hicks as too liberal, but who were nevertheless concerned to preserve old Quaker ways from innovation. To their ears, Gurney's message sounded far too close to Episcopal or Methodist doctrine, too far from the old-time emphasis on the Inner Light.

In New England, a stout defender of the old-time Quaker faith had appeared in the person of John Wilbur of Hopkinton, Rhode Island. Born in 1774, Wilbur was a schoolteacher of humble origins and modest circumstances. He is described as a kindly and affectionate man, but he was stubborn and persistent in guarding "the old inheritance" against the new ideas.

As a recorded minister, Wilbur traveled in England from 1831 to 1833. Here he became convinced that Joseph Gurney was a threat to the concept of the Inner Light, and that it was his mission to defend Friends against the latest machinations of the devil. He preached throughout England against "departure," sat in weeping silence through London Yearly Meeting, and wrote a series of "Letters to a Friend on some of the Primitive Doctrines of Christianity," which were published and became the basis of fresh doctrinal disputes.

When Gurney came to the United States, a few years later, Wilbur followed him about, attempting to influence people against his doctrines. He was determined, but no match for the oratory or the charm of the polished Englishman. Even New England Yearly Meeting itself came strongly under the Gurney influence. Finding Wilbur an increasing embarrassment, this body attempted in 1843 to disown him.

A complicated struggle between the quarterly, monthly, and yearly meetings developed which resulted in a separation in 1845. About five hundred members left New England Yearly Meeting to rally around Wilbur, while sixty-five hundred remained in the fold.

Rival claims between "the smaller body" and "the large body," to be recognized by the other yearly meetings, led once more to further splits. In Ohio, still profoundly wounded by the bitter separation of 1828, a Wilburite-Gurneyite separation occurred in 1854. In Philadelphia, a similar schism was narrowly averted. Rather than risk separation over the issue Philadelphia decided to recognize no other yearly meetings. For many years Philadelphia maintained its unity through virtual isolation from the rest of the Society.

The Wilburite-Gurneyite separation was a fresh tragedy to the Quakers. Once more there were lawsuits contesting meeting and school property; once more families were split by bitter feelings. Men and women kept their faces averted as they drove their buggies past rival meetinghouses, and cousins avoided each other.

Strongly evangelical in doctrine, the Gurneyite meetings in the Midwest were particularly susceptible to the evangelical revivals that swept the frontier in the years after the Civil War. With the help of the evangelists, they felt they regained the reality in religion they had lost during the long years of dullness. Once the immediate excitement of the revival was over, however, these meetings found they were unable to maintain the religious fervor they had experienced without the help of a pastor. Many began to hire visiting evangelists to stay on, or to pay a local farmer or teacher with a gift for the ministry to serve as pastor part-time. Finally they began to hire full-time pastors as do other Protestant churches.

This shift to a pastoral system alarmed a group of conservative Friends in the Midwest, and led to the creation of a group of Conservative Yearly Meetings in the 1870's in Iowa, Indiana, and Kansas. A Conservative Yearly Meeting was established in Canada in 1881 and in North Carolina in 1903. The Conservatives maintain the silent meeting, and have been the last to give up the plain dress and plain speech of their ancestors.

Among the Gurneyite meetings which developed a pastoral system there occurred a further division. A large group of these meetings attempted to stay close to the original Quaker message by maintaining a period of silence as part of the worship service and by keeping in close touch with London Yearly Meeting. In 1902, these meetings banded together to form the Five Years Meeting of Friends, now called the Friends United Meeting. Today Friends United Meeting is the largest single body of Friends in the United States, and embraces many variations of belief and practices.

Dissenting from this group on the grounds of creed are four yearly meetings: Ohio, Kansas, Oregon, and Rocky Mountain, which now form the Evangelical Friends Alliance. Some of these meetings have returned to the use of the sacraments of baptism and communion, and most of them take an essentially fundamentalist view of the Bible.

Schisms within the Society of Friends throughout the nineteenth century influenced other aspects of Quaker history. On such issues as the abolition of slavery, the conduct of the Underground Railroad, the establishment of liberal arts colleges, the development of foreign missions, the Quakers of that era tended to take sides along the lines of separations.

Fortunately, the twentieth century has seen a reversal in the trend of schism. The creation of the Five Years Meeting was a step toward reuniting, followed by the rejoining of the Hicksites and the Orthodox in 1955. All the yearly meetings have cooperated at times in the support of such groups as the American Friends Service Committee. In the past forty years a group of new and united meetings have been developed, mainly on college campuses, which have ignored the divisions of the past. Scattered from the East Coast to the West, these new meetings are serving as bridges between the differing groups.

Despite the sad history of separations, the Quaker Movement continued to change and develop throughout the nineteenth century. Its saving grace was its deep concern for social problems outside the narrow confines of its own society. Just as the withdrawal from the world following the Revolutionary War triggered the long series of schisms, so a deepening involvement and responsible concern have helped with reuniting and healing. The deepest concern during the past century was the abolition of slavery.

# 6

# The abolition
# of slavery

One of the trademarks of the Quakers has been their
insistence upon equality regardless of race, creed, and national
origin. This concern goes back a long way. The world's first
declaration against slavery was made by the Quakers of Germantown in 1688. In that year the Germantown Monthly Meeting,
under the leadership of Daniel Pastorius, sent up to Philadelphia
Yearly Meeting a celebrated protest:

> There is a liberty of conscience here which is right and rea-
> sonable, and there ought to be likewise a liberty of the body,
> except for evil doers, which is another case. But to bring men

hither, or to rob and sell them against their will, we stand against.

It took the Quakers many years to live up to this first protest. Many shared in the antislavery sentiment from the beginning, but some not only owned slaves, but were partners in the importing of slaves. Because of the need to achieve unity, the Society as a whole could not move ahead of its more conservative members. It was not until 1784, almost one hundred years after the Germantown declaration, that the last Quakers agreed to free their slaves. Yet they were the first religious body not only to do this, but to espouse abolition as a state and national policy. Through the troubled nineteenth century, Friends were active in the antislavery movement, the Underground Railroad, and the welfare of freed slaves after the Civil War. Today Quakers are still working to make opportunity equal for all.

Because of the presence of some conservative members, Philadelphia Yearly Meeting was at first unable to take any action on the Germantown declaration at all. Eight years later, the group finally agreed upon a careful minute advising Friends not to encourage the importation of more slaves. There matters rested until 1700, when the Quaker-dominated Pennsylvania Assembly enacted a law prohibiting the importation of Negroes into the colony. The Royal Council in Great Britain promptly rejected this law. Next year, when the Assembly tried instead to levy a twenty-pound duty on every slave imported, the Queen annulled their action.

At about this time groups within the Yearly Meeting began to press for a ruling against individual Quakers purchasing imported slaves. Between 1711 and 1729 Chester Meeting, a center of antislavery sentiment, sent at least five memorials to Philadelphia urging this. At last in 1739 Philadelphia made the purchase of imported slaves a cause for disownment. At the same time the Yearly Meeting advised Friends to take good care of those Negroes they possessed through inheritance.

The next step was to persuade Quakers to give up the slaves they now owned. Since slaves constituted a valuable form of property in those days this was the equivalent of persuading modern Quakers—or Baptists, or Presbyterians—to give away inherited stocks or real estate, or the family car. Although the yearly meetings gradually grew stricter and stricter on this point, encouraging individual Friends to give up their property, it had to be done on a one-by-one basis. This was accomplished throughout the Society of Friends in the period before the Revolutionary War by a handful of dedicated individuals. Thomas Hazard of Rhode Island broke with his wealthy, slave-owning father to press antislavery sentiment throughout New England. Anthony Benezet led the battle in Philadelphia, and established the first school for Negro children in that city. Benjamin Lay, an eccentric dwarf, roused many Friends from their lethargy with his fiery speeches.

It was John Woolman, however, who chiefly awakened the Friends in America to the need to clear themselves of slave-owning. A simple tailor from Mount Holly, New Jersey, Woolman was one of the finest flowers of Quakerism. His *Journal,* written with an artless and limpid simplicity, is read as a literary classic. It is also perhaps the finest exposition of Quakerism, revealing as it does one man's struggle to open himself fully to the dictates of the Inner Light. His social concerns—for the ending of slavery, for the Indians, for peace—flow as naturally as water from his inner concentration on keeping open and humble.

Woolman was born in 1720 in the little community of Rancocas, New Jersey, on the lovely Rancocas River. The oldest son in a family of thirteen children, he grew up a quiet and serious little boy, who enjoyed books and the simple education he received at the nearby Quaker school. During his teens he experienced a period of restlessness when "to excel in the art of foolish jesting and to promote mirth were my chief study," but by the age of twenty he was wholly concentrated on leading a godly life.

Although he loved nature, John Woolman did not care particularly for the life of a farmer. Instead, when he was a young man he went to Mount Holly to work for a local merchant, arranging to be taught the tailoring trade by another employee. Later he established his own shop, where he both sewed garments and handled merchandise. In after years he gave up a good part of his shopkeeping, since he believed that too much "cumber" kept a man from total concentration on the life of the spirit. He married at twenty-nine, and had only two children. One son died in infancy. His wife and daughter were glad to live simply so that Woolman might be free to follow the leadings of the Inner Light.

John Woolman's testimony against slavery first took shape in his mind when his employer in Mount Holly asked him to draw up a bill of sale for a Negro woman. Woolman, always sensitive, felt torn between doing what he suddenly saw to be wrong and hurting the feelings of his kind master and the equally kind Quaker who was buying the slave. In the end he wrote the bill, but he felt compelled to tell both the other men that he felt slavery to be wrong. From that time on, however, he refused to participate in such sales, or to write wills in which the inheritance of slaves was involved. Instead, he used these occasions to remonstrate gently with the slave owners in question.

In 1746 Woolman, now a recognized minister, decided to travel south with another Friend on a religious mission. The condition in which the slaves lived in Maryland and in Virginia upset him very much, and he was unhappy about receiving hospitality from slave owners who lived in idle luxury on the labor of their Negroes. The condition of the white southerners worried him too.

> I saw so many vices and corruptions in a great measure occasioned by this trade and way of life, that it appears to me as a dark gloominess hanging over the land . . . in future the consequences will be grievous to posterity.

On his return from this trip he wrote an essay, "Some Considerations on the Keeping of Negroes." He showed it to his family, but with characteristic modesty made no effort to get it published. When Woolman's father lay on his deathbed four years later he brought up the question of the manuscript, and asked his gifted son to offer it to the overseers of the Quaker Press. This led to its publication in 1754.

The year following his southern trip, John Woolman traveled in New England, reinforcing the antislavery work of Thomas Hazard. The importing of slaves was still a big business in Rhode Island, and Friends were not clear of it, nor of the ownership of slaves. This troubled Woolman very much and sharpened his testimony against slave-owning. He returned to New England in 1760, and on this second trip persuaded Friends to offer a memorial to the legislature outlawing the slave trade. On this second trip also he visited with Quaker ministers and elders one by one, urging them to relinquish their slaves.

Meanwhile, Woolman's growing concern to end slavery sent him south on a second mission in 1757. This time he took along a bag of silver coins and whenever he felt he had received hospitality at the expense of the slave system he paid his host, or the Negro servants, for his room and board. He dreaded these embarrassing parting interviews very much, but such was his sweetness, and his real concern for the welfare of the slave owner as well as the slave, that he managed to get through them without an exchange of angry words.

Shortly after his return from this second southern trip, Woolman attended the Philadelphia Yearly Meeting. Here, the question of the immediate freeing of slaves was once more discussed. The general sentiment of the Meeting seemed to be again that the time was not yet ripe for such drastic action. Then Woolman spoke out of the agony of his recent trip through the South, and galvanized the Yearly Meeting with his heartfelt eloquence. A minute urging members to give up their slaves was passed and a committee appointed to visit the slaveholders individually and to persuade them to surrender their human property. For two years John Woolman served on that committee, using a warm and gentle persuasion that few could finally resist.

Other concerns gripped John Woolman at this same period. In 1755 he was one of a group of Quakers who stated their opposition to the payment of war taxes. In 1758 he was ordered to accept two soldiers as boarders in his Mount Holly home. After deep thought he agreed to take them, but not to accept money for their board. In the end only one soldier came, and he stayed only two weeks. In the Woolman household he rapidly shed his rough ways, helped with chores, and played with Woolman's little daughter. Nevertheless, John Woolman felt he could not accept the money the captain offered him at the soldier's departure, and made a special trip to visit the captain at his home and explain why.

He supported the young conscientious objectors to war of his day, yet his sensitivity and fair mindedness made him look at the problem of handling the few CO's who misbehaved from the point of view of the officer:

> Among the officers are men of understanding, who have some regard to sincerity when they see it and in the execution of their office when they have men to deal with whom they be-

lieve to be upright hearted, to put them to the trouble on account of scruples of conscience is a painful task, likely to be avoided as easily as may be. But where men profess to be meek and heavenly minded, and to have their trust firmly settled in God that they cannot join in wars, and yet by their spirit and conduct in common life manifest a contrary disposition, their difficulties are great at such a time.

Though not as involved in work for the Indians as his friend Anthony Benezet or Israel Pemberton, John Woolman helped to found the New Jersey Association for Helping the Indians and attended an Indian-Quaker peace conference. As he brooded about a recent French and Indian war, and its causes in human greed, he decided to make a personal trip to see Chief Papunehaung and to visit among the Indians, "that I might feel and understand their life and the spirit they live in, if haply I might receive some instruction from them, or they might in any degree be helped forward by my following the leadings of Truth among them." In the spring of 1763 he set out, against the strong objections of his fellow Quakers and his family, since the Indians were on the warpath. Nevertheless, he had a safe journey and several meetings for meditation with the Indians. At the end of one of these, Chief Papunehaung is reported to have said: "I love to feel where words come from," as good an interpretation as any of the root-experience of Quaker worship.

As John Woolman grew older, he became more and more convinced that the root of war, slavery, and every social evil lay in greed and ownership of excessive property. He developed an obsession to free himself from supporting human misery through his use of items of luxury paid for by slaves. Believing that the dye industry rested heavily on slavery, he began to wear only undyed clothes. Later, he refused to eat with silver in the homes of his friends. On a trip to England he traveled steerage, rather than escape the conditions of the common sailors by sleeping in the cabin with his Quaker companions. In England, he walked from town to town, believing that the stage boys and the horses were both abused by the interest in too much speed.

These eccentricities were acceptable to those who knew and loved John Woolman, but to strangers they were something of a shock. When the strange-looking Woolman arrived at London Yearly Meeting in 1772, planning to travel as a minister throughout England, a weighty Friend arose and suggested that Woolman might feel his mission completed and himself at liberty to return home again. This so hurt the New Jersey mystic that he wept. Then rising, he agreed that he would not travel unless the Meeting felt unity with him, but that he would wait until this time and support himself as a tailor. Later in the Meeting he was moved to speak again, and this time was so eloquent and moving that the weighty Quaker apologized for his rudeness and the Meeting agreed to Woolman's traveling.

Tragically enough, this trip marked the end of Woolman's life. Whether worn-out by the long hard voyage in the steerage, or by the long tramp through the English countryside, Woolman was not in good health that summer. In September, while visiting in York, he fell ill with smallpox, a disease he had dreaded all his life. After eight days of suffering he died, and was buried far from his home and his beloved Rancocas.

John Woolman's great friend, Anthony Benezet, is chiefly known for the letters and pamphlets he poured forth throughout his lifetime, attacking the institution of slavery. He was far more outspoken and blunt than the gentle Woolman, but his eloquence was often effective in arousing the lukewarm. Many of the men active in opposing slavery during this period were first awakened to action by Benezet. In addition, the little schoolmaster, who was himself French in origin, took personal charge of providing relief for the French-speaking refugees from Nova Scotia (the subject of Longfellow's poem, "Evangeline") during their protracted stay in Philadelphia. He was active in work for the Indians, and for many years taught a school for Negroes. Out of this experience came perhaps the first statement on educational equality for the races:

> I have found amongst Negroes as great a variety of talents as among a like number of whites, and I am bold to assert that the notion entertained by some that blacks are inferior in their capacities is a vulgar prejudice, founded on the pride and ignorance of their lordly masters, who have kept their slaves at such a distance as to be unable to form a right judgment of them.

Having finally rid the Society of Friends of complicity in slaveholding, Friendly reformers turned to the task of abolishing slavery throughout the land. On April 14, 1775, just four days before Paul Revere's famous ride, a group of Philadelphia's leading citizens, including many Quakers, met at Sun Tavern to form the world's first abolition society, "The Pennsylvania Society for Promoting the Abolition of Slavery, the Relief of Negroes Unlawfully Held in Bondage, and for Improving the Conditions of the African Race." It was active in its early years in pressing both the state and nation toward abolition, and in stimulating the creation of other abolition societies. In 1780, Pennsylvania outlawed slavery, an outcome for which the Society worked hard in its early years, and in 1808 the United States passed a law outlawing the importation of slaves, partly as a result of pressure from all the infant abolition societies under Pennsylvania's leadership.

The Society of Friends came to regard the participation of individual Quakers in such an organization as the Pennsylvania

Abolition Society as something decidedly questionable. With the growing withdrawal of Quakers from public life in the period following the Revolutionary War, the activity of Friends in "mixed" societies came more and more under criticism. As the abolitionist movement gained momentum and heat, the conservative elements in the Society were particularly alarmed by the involvement of their coreligionists in antislavery activities. Friends were advised to "stay in the quiet" and not to mix in worldly affairs.

Quakers were undoubtedly united in feeling that slavery was a great evil. If a thousand John Woolmans could have been found to fan out throughout the country, changing the hearts of men, all Friends would have been agreed that this was a proper approach. As it was, some Friends felt it was best not to be involved in activities which might lead to violence (indeed the Civil War realized their worst fears), while others felt the evils of slavery could not be left to time but must be dealt with immediately. Some of the liberals suspected that the wealthy Quaker merchants of the East who urged a go-slow policy had a financial stake in the stability of the South.

Even among those Friends who were bent on active participation in reform movements, there were differences of opinion about means. In 1816, the American Colonization Society was organized for the purpose of settling free Negroes in Africa, the West Indies, and other places. Some Quakers opposed the Society from the start, calling it a palliative, designed to remove free slaves from the country and thus reduce the incentive of others to seek their freedom. Others supported it as a means to induce slaveholders to give up their slaves.

Among supporters of the Colonization Society was Benjamin Lundy, a Quaker from New Jersey who migrated to Mount Pleasant, Ohio, and there formed an antislavery society called the

"Union Human Society." Lundy wrote articles for the *Philan-thropist,* an antislavery journal published by another Quaker, Charles Osborn, and later published a journal of his own, *The Genius of Universal Emancipation.* In the interests of the Colo-nization Society, he traveled to Canada, Texas, Mexico, and Haiti, looking for homes for the freed slaves. One of his projects was finding a place to resettle 729 slaves given by their masters to the North Carolina Meeting to hold until they could be conveyed to a land of freedom. Possibly his most notable achievement was the enlisting of William Lloyd Garrison in the antislavery move-ment.

In 1833 a meeting was held in Philadelphia to form the American Anti-Slavery Society. William Lloyd Garrison presided, and at his side was his young protégé, the New England poet John Greenleaf Whittier. Though women were excluded from partici-pation in this meeting, a group of Philadelphia ladies concerned about slavery were invited to attend as onlookers. In the midst of this group in the gallery sat a beautiful young Quaker matron. It was Lucretia Mott's first formal introduction to the antislavery movement.

A member of the prominent Quaker family, the Coffins of Nantucket, Lucretia was a promising student from the day she started school. At Nine-Partners Boarding School near Pough-keepsie, where she went at the age of twelve, she was the leading girl student. At the age of fifteen she was named an assistant teacher, though as a mere woman she received no salary. There were other compensations, however. She had an opportunity to learn French, which she later taught, and she had a chance to become better acquainted with James Mott, the tall, blond young man who was the senior teacher at the school.

In 1811 the Motts were married, and set up housekeeping in Philadelphia. James Mott became a merchant, and after a few early hardships became moderately successful. Lucretia taught school between babies when times were hard, but preferred to devote herself to her home, her children, and the life of her Quaker meeting. She showed early promise in the ministry, and was recognized officially as a minister in 1821, when she was only twenty-eight years of age.

The serene life of the Philadelphia Motts was first interrupted by the troubles within the Philadelphia Yearly Meeting. Having known Elias Hicks as a minister who often visited Nine-Partners School, and as a staunch enemy of slavery, James and Lucretia felt sympathetic toward him, and indignant about the efforts of the elders to quiet him. In 1827, when the split finally came, James Mott became a Hicksite, and Lucretia followed him almost a year later. Regretfully they withdrew their daughter from Westtown Boarding School, which remained under the control of the Orthodox wing.

James and Lucretia Mott were strongly against slavery from the beginning of their married life. Shortly after James Mott became an established merchant he decided he could no longer handle cotton from the slave states, and thereafter restricted his merchandise to different forms of wool. Lucretia heartily agreed with her husband's decision, though at first it cut down their income. She supported the "Free Produce" movement in her home by using no articles that were made with slave labor. Artificially sweetened candy, contained in little nuggets called "prize packages," were the Mott children's only sweets.

After the meeting of the Anti-Slavery Society in Philadelphia, Lucretia Mott organized the Philadelphia Female Anti-Slavery Society, and later was one of the leaders of the Anti-Slavery Convention of American Women, inaugurated at an assembly held in New York in May, 1837. In 1840, when the General Conference of British and Foreign Anti-Slavery Societies was

called in London, James and Lucretia Mott were named as two
of the five delegates from the United States.

By the mid 1830's, public sentiment in many northern cities
had hardened against the abolitionists. The fact that some of
these abolitionists were women—daring to speak to mixed gatherings—upset tempers still further. Between 1835 and 1845 there
were frequent outbreaks of mob violence against antislavery
leaders. In Philadelphia the beautiful new Pennsylvania Hall,
dedicated to "Liberty and the Rights of Man," was burned in
1838 by an angry mob in the midst of the second meeting of the
Anti-Slavery Convention of American Women. John Greenleaf
Whittier, who had just established his office in the new hall as
editor of the *Pennsylvania Freeman,* was able to save a few
precious manuscripts by disguising himself and slipping through
the angry crowd. Later, the mob turned with a cry "on to the
Motts." Lucretia and James, sitting at home with a few loyal
friends, calmly awaited their arrival, but other friends of the
Motts managed to distract the crowd by shouting "on to the
Motts" and pointing in the wrong direction.

Strong sentiment against the meddling of women eventually
led to a tragic split in the abolitionist movement. The new
group, including Whittier, preferred not to mix the issues of
slavery and of women's rights. When she went with her husband
to the world antislavery conference in London in 1840 Lucretia
Mott found herself barred from attending the session because the
international group took the same view. Excluded along with her
were three other American women, Sarah Pugh, Abby Kimber,
and Anne Phillips. A fourth American, Elizabeth Cady Stanton,
the wife of Henry B. Stanton, was not herself a delegate, but
sympathized with the excluded women and sat with them
throughout the conference.

From this meeting grew a decision on the part of Lucretia

Mott and Elizabeth Stanton to hold a Women's Rights Convention. The resulting conference, organized in Seneca Falls in 1848, marks the beginning of the women's rights movements in the United States. Lucretia took an active part in this work throughout her lifetime, and was referred to frequently as a "lion" in the cause. Contemporary accounts, however, paint her as very different from the usual feminist stereotype. A diminutive and gentle person, she was devoted to her home and family, kept house for many years for an expanded family group of twelve, thought nothing of entertaining as many as thirty for dinner, cooked, sewed, knitted, gardened, and cleaned with vigor and enjoyment. Whenever she had time to sit and chat, her hands were busy with knitting, mending, or rolling balls of rags for carpets.

As she grew older, Lucretia Mott's interests branched out. She was active in the newly formed Peace Society, the temperance movement, the efforts to establish public schools, the development of a workshop for "fallen" women. She helped establish Swarthmore College, of which her husband James was an incorporator, and she was actively involved in the development of schools for the freed slaves after the Civil War. In and out of the abolition movement she had Negro friends, and she entertained them in mixed groups with a grace from which modern liberals might learn a thing or two.

Throughout her life Lucretia was active in the meetings and the committee work of the Society of Friends. However, as her gifts as a minister developed, she was also much in demand to preach to the Unitarians, just then throwing off the yoke of Calvinist doctrine. She was a friend of many of the Transcendentalists of the day, including Ralph Waldo Emerson, and a member of the Free Religious Association. This interest, which alarmed her fellow Quakers, was based on her belief that the scripture should not be accepted blindly, but subjected to logic, and that everyone should have freedom of religious expression. She herself never wavered in her Quaker faith in the Inner Light and her Quaker habit of translating that Light into immediate and practical action. She narrowly escaped being disowned, once for her abolitionist activities and once for her "heresy," but lived to a grand old age as a Friend, and attended Philadelphia Yearly Meeting just before she died.

Another famous Quaker abolitionist of the day was Whittier. A birthright Friend, John Greenleaf Whittier was born in Haverhill, Massachusetts, in 1807. He had a meager education, but began writing poetry when he was still in his early teens. One of his poems was seen by William Lloyd Garrison, then editor of the *Newburyport Free Press.* The great abolitionist became interested in the boy, and encouraged him to complete his education. After graduation from Haverhill Academy, Whittier took a job as editor of the *American Manufacturer,* continuing to write poetry on the side. He moved on to become the editor of the *Essex Gazette* in 1830, and the *Pennsylvania Freeman* in 1838.

An ardent abolitionist, Whittier took the position that no other causes, laudable though they might be, should be mixed with the antislavery movement. In 1837, when the abolitionist forces divided, he went with "the new Society," splitting with both his former benefactor, Garrison, and his fellow Quaker, Lucretia Mott. He objected to Garrison's desire to mix the women's rights issue into the antislavery issue, to the former's disdain for political action as a means of achieving emancipation, and to his avowed indifference to the preservation of the Union.

Whittier himself was deeply interested in politics, and abandoned a promising political career to throw himself into the abolitionist cause. He was eventually successful in interjecting the issue of emancipation into national politics and helped form the Liberty party, and later the Republican party.

Plagued all his life by ill health, Whittier was unable to attend the London Conference on Abolition in 1840, and had to retire from an active role from that time on. Instead, he wrote moving poetry which helped to awaken the conscience of a nation. "Countrymen in Chains" is a famous example:

> Our fellow countrymen in chains!
>> Slaves—in a land of light and law!—
> Slaves—crouching on the very plains
>> Where rolled the storm of Freedom's war!
> A groan from Eutaw's haunted wood—
>> A wail where Camden's martyrs fell—
> By every shrine of patriot blood,
>> From Moultrie's wall and Jasper's well! . . . .
>
> Just God! and shall we calmly rest,
>> The Christian's scorn—the heathen's mirth—
> Content to live the lingering jest
>> And by-word of a mocking earth?
> Shall our own glorious land retain
>> That curse which Europe scorns to bear?
> Shall our own brethren drag the chain
>> Which not even Russia's menials wear? . . . .
>
> Prone let the shrine of Moloch sink,
>> And leave no traces where it stood—
> Nor longer let its idol drink
>> His daily cup of human blood:
> But rear another altar there,
>> To truth and love and mercy given,
> And Freedom's gift and Freedom's prayer
>> Shall call an answer down from Heaven!

Whittier also aided the Underground movement in both Philadelphia and New York, and traveled with the great English abolitionist Joseph Sturge, when the latter made a lecture tour of the United States. When the New England Yearly Meeting refused the Englishman the use of their meetinghouses for anti-slavery addresses, Whittier decided to stop participating in Yearly Meeting activities.

Earlier Whittier had complained of the conservatism of Quakers on the slavery issue. In 1837 he wrote in the *Freeman:*

> . . . they have done well in times past, but we fear that at the present crisis they are, as a body, too lukewarm for this subject. Their ancient and excellent testimony against slavery has been, in too many instances, sacrificed to prejudice, mercantile connections with slaveholders, and a somewhat inconsistent dread of association with other sects for any other purposes than those of worldy gain.

Whittier was nevertheless very proud to be a Quaker, and much of his poetry celebrated events in Quaker history: "The King's Missive," "Cassandra Southwick," "The Exiles," "The Meeting," and "The Quaker Alumni." When asked if he thought he was going too far in his fearless espousal of the abolitionist cause, he replied that he could always retreat into his Quakerism like a turtle into its shell.

At the outbreak of the Civil War he felt, like Lucretia Mott, that he could not condone violence even if it was being used to a good end. He urged his fellow Quakers to be nurses to the wounded, and himself too ill to serve, helped them raise money for the cause. A pithy story illustrates his somewhat mixed feelings about the war. Traveling in New Hampshire, Whittier met a fellow Quaker on his way to Kittery, Maine, to sell his lumber to a shipyard. Whittier told the Friend that he was undoubtedly entering into a war contract, and gave him a lecture about the violation of principle involved. At the end however he added, "If thee does furnish any of the timber thee spoke of, be sure it is all sound." The Friend went through with the sale, and his lumber formed the hull of the *Kearsarge,* a famous Union battleship.

After the war Whittier retired from public life and devoted himself to writing. "Snowbound" sold so well that he was at last financially comfortable. Some of his religious poems, written during this period, were subsequently adapted as hymns and are still widely sung throughout the United States. His health kept him from traveling, but he maintained a correspondence with people all over the world, which gave him great pleasure. He died in 1892, at the age of eighty-five, having earned himself the title of "Quaker Poet."

Active abolitionists like Lucretia Mott and John Greenleaf Whittier were in the minority within the Society of Friends. Alarmed by the violence which began to crop up in the middle 1830's around the abolitionist cause, the Quakers went through a period of disciplining and in a few cases disowning Friends who were too active. In Indiana, where abolitionist feelings became particularly intense, a separation occurred, and a new body of Anti-Slavery Friends, numbering some two thousand members, was established. Elsewhere smaller splits occurred.

No issues aroused livelier debate within the Society of Friends at this period than the question of participation in the Underground Railroad. This was the system by which escaping slaves were passed on from friendly hands to friendly hands until they reached Canada and safety. The Quakers never officially sponsored the Underground Railroad, but many individuals played a prominent role in the movement throughout the country. One Friend, Levi Coffin of Cincinnati, was called the President of the Underground Railroad, having helped some one hundred slaves escape each year for twenty years.

Conservative members of the Society of Friends worried about these activities because they had to be conducted in secret, and because they were often illegal. Until this time Friends had prided themselves on doing everything in an aboveboard fashion, and in maintaining a reputation for strict honesty. The ones who participated felt that the immorality of slavery was so great that a higher morality forced them to combat it with the means at hand. They remained truthful, but the demands of the situation resulted in some splitting of hairs. A Quaker farming couple, asked if there were any runaway slaves on their premises, said, "there are no slaves here," meaning they did not recognize that any person could be a slave. A deaf grandfather hid an escaped slave in his wagonload of brooms, ordered his grandson, who normally served as his interpreter, to hide too, and then was truthfully able to say he could hear not one word when the federal officer detained him to ask him about the runaway.

One of the outstanding figures of the Underground Railroad was Isaac Hopper, a peppery Philadelphia Quaker noted for his physical likeness to Napoleon. Isaac came from New Jersey. but moved to Philadelphia at the age of sixteen to become a tailor's apprentice. Shortly after coming to the City of Brotherly Love he had a chance to help a runaway slave from Bermuda find safety. He was so moved by the former slave's situation, and subsequent gratitude, that he began to seek opportunities to perform similar services. Soon he was known throughout the Philadelphia area as the man to whom to turn whenever a Negro was in trouble.

Although he was not a trained lawyer, Hopper became intimately acquainted with the laws governing slaves. He learned that if a slave spent six months on the free soil of Pennsylvania with his master's knowledge he could proclaim his own freedom and refuse to return south with his master. He also learned to beware of slave-catchers, who sometimes kidnaped free northern Negroes and took them south to sell them, or fraudulently claim that they were someone's lost slave.

Isaac Hopper was absolutely fearless. One day a Negro woman

Isaac Hopper. (*Courtesy the Quaker Collection, Haverford College Library. Photo by Norman Wilson.*)

came to his house in great distress to say that her ten-year-old son had been taken aboard a ship bound for Baltimore. Hopper rushed to the dock, and finding that the boat had already set sail, rushed home again, got his fastest horse, and galloped down to Gloucester Point. Here he persuaded the ferry owner to intercept the packet. The captain, thinking it was another passenger, allowed Hopper to climb aboard. When the little Quaker reached the deck and stated his business, however, the master of the ship was not disposed to interfere with the slave-catcher. Characteristically, Hopper at this point whipped out a book of Pennsylvania law and read the penalties the captain would incur the next time he touched on Pennsylvania soil, if he continued to resist the rescue of the boy.

Though the captain at this point stood aside, the kidnapper was another matter. Since the rest of the passengers and most of the crew sided against Hopper, the rescue of the Negro boy was difficult. The Quaker was not willing to fight, but he used his body as a shield to fend off blows while the boy jumped into the waiting arms of the ferryman below. Then, after a considerable struggle, Hopper was able to disentangle himself and leap from the deck into the ferry without injury. A swift run for shore, and the rescue was accomplished. Hopper had literally hundreds of such adventures in his lifetime. Whatever hour of the day and night, he was ready to leap from his bed or his trade to answer the call of anxious and frightened Negroes.

Hopper married twice, and both wives gave him a large number of children. His was a warm and happy home life, all members of his family sharing a great pride in his gallantry. Unfortunately the Hoppers were usually in straitened circumstances, Isaac's devotion to the cause interfering seriously with his ability to earn a living. In 1829, in an effort to improve his financial situation, he moved to New York City where he ran a Quaker bookshop, worked as bookkeeper for the Anti-Slavery Society, and later became secretary of the Prison Association.

Throughout these years he continued to be deeply concerned about the abolition of slavery, and helped promote a paper called the *Anti-Slavery Standard*. A dispute which arose within the Society of Friends over an antislavery editorial in this paper led to his disownment in 1842 along with two other Friends. Wrote L. Maria Childs, an abolitionist and Hopper's contemporary biographer, "A Society has need to be very rich in moral excellence that they can afford to throw away three such members." A fellow Hicksite commented wryly, "Well, it appears that the persecuted have now, in their turn, become persecutors." Though several of his children resigned from the Society of Friends in protest, Hopper himself seemed to bear his meeting no ill will and attended regularly until he died.

Another Quaker of a Robin Hood cast was Thomas Garrett of Wilmington, Delaware. When Thomas was eighteen, a free Negro woman named Nancy who worked for the Garrett family was kidnapped by slave-catchers. Thomas rescued her in person, and was so touched by her gratitude that he then and there decided to devote his life to work for the freedom of slaves. Altogether he is supposed to have helped twenty-seven hundred slaves on their way to freedom, without one ever being recaptured. In 1848 a civil case was tried against him in Delaware and such heavy damages were awarded that he lost everything he owned. Garrett is supposed to have said, "Judge, thou hast not left me a dollar, but if anyone knows of a fugitive who wants a shelter and a friend send him to Thomas Garrett and he will befriend him." His many loyal friends raised capital with which again to make him solvent, and until the outbreak of the Civil War he continued to work against slavery.

Levi Coffin, the "President of the Underground Railroad" came from the Quaker colony in New Garden, North Carolina. While still a very young man he and a cousin organized a station of the Underground Railroad which met in the pine thickets on the edge of town. In 1826 he migrated to Wayne County, Indiana. Here his home, located at the converging point of three Underground Railroad systems from the South, became one of the most successful and one of the most famous stations in the entire network of lines connecting the South and the North. An average of one hundred passengers a year stopped at the Coffins. He writes:

> Seldom a week passed without our receiving passengers by this mysterious road. We found it necessary to be always prepared to receive company and probably to care for them. We knew not what night or what hour of the night we would be roused from slumber by a gentle rap at the door. That was the signal announcing the arrival of a train of the Underground Railroad, for the locomotive did not whistle or make any unnecessary noise.

By 1845, the rifts between the abolitionist Friends and the rest of the Society began to heal, and the Society of Friends as a whole became more and more identified nationally with the cause of emancipation. Though dreading the potential conflict they foresaw, the Quakers were convinced that there was no way out through colonization or any other scheme, and they put their faith more and more with Whittier in political action.

When at last the mounting tensions broke, the Civil War brought a time of severe trial to the Quakers and their peace testimony. Like Whittier, many Friends were torn between their testimony against violence and their belief that in this war justice was predominantly on one side. Abraham Lincoln, who claimed Quaker ancestry, put the problem succinctly in a letter he wrote Eliza Gurney, widow of Joseph John Gurney:

> Your people, the Friends, have had and are having a very great trial. On principle and faith, opposed to both war and oppression, they can only practically oppose oppression by war. In

this dilemma some have chosen one horn of the dilemma and some the other. For those appealing to me on conscientious grounds I have done, and shall do, what I could and can in my own conscience under my oath to the law. That you believe this I doubt not, and believing it, I shall receive for our country and myself your earnest prayers to our Father in Heaven.

Your sincere friend,
A. LINCOLN

In her reply, Eliza Gurney refused to admit that a true Friend could choose the second horn of the dilemma. Nevertheless, some did. Perhaps two or three hundred young Quakers in all enlisted in the Union army, the largest number coming from Indiana. One regiment, the 15th Pennsylvania, was led by a Hicksite Friend, Colonel John Palmer, and was known as the Quaker regiment because many of its officers and men were also Quakers. A few older Quakers helped with war supplies. Secretary of War Edwin Stanton was the son of a Quaker. Both he and Lincoln were lenient toward Quaker conscientious objectors, and their enemies described them as belonging to "The Quaker War Cabinet."

Nevertheless, the great majority of Quakers remained steadfast to their peace testimony. Some meetings disowned their fighting members, and the various yearly meetings refused to participate in enforcing the draft. Young Quakers were conscientious objectors, and their elders refused to pay war taxes. At least one Quaker manufacturer, Horatio Wood, refused to allow his blanket factory to be used to produce blankets for the Union army. Instead, it was taken over by the government.

During the war, Quakers devoted themselves to nursing and to taking care of the "contraband," the recently freed slaves who congregated in large numbers behind Union lines. Quaker women sewed and patched garments for the freedmen. Quaker men raised money for their food and shelter. Young Friends went south to work among them. English and Irish Friends sent generous contributions toward the cause.

The Draft Act of 1863 forced many young Quakers to make a decision about the war effort. At first the draft was so laxly administered that few Quakers were involved, but by the end of the war several had been arrested and imprisoned for refusal to serve. Three young Quakers from Vermont had a particularly rough time. They were drafted and then disciplined severely by army officers for their refusal to carry guns, or even perform medical work in lieu of military service. One of the boys was finally stretched out on the ground by an angry officer and spread-eagled, with each hand and foot tied to a stake, then left, first in the broiling sun, then in the rain, until he should change his mind. After several days in which this torture was repeated he was released, Friends in Washington having brought his case to the attention of Lincoln. All three Vermont boys were subsequently paroled home.

At about this time the Congress passed a second draft act, exempting religious objectors from military service, provided they either did medical work, helped with the freedmen, or paid $300 into a fund to be used for the freedmen. Some Quakers accepted this alternative service, or paid the fee, but the eastern yearly meetings did not approve of the procedure. There were still some absolute objectors, whom Lincoln dealt with by paroling them home.

In the South, the Quakers had a more difficult time. Many migrated west during this time, and those that remained were regarded as abolitionists and traitors by their southern neighbors. This hostility, plus the extreme shortage of men throughout the South, resulted in a great deal of pressure on southern conscientious objectors. Members of the historic peace churches, Friends, Dunkards, Nazarenes, and Mennonites, were exempted from the draft on the payment of a $500 fee, but not many Quakers felt free to accept this way out, or alternative service, which was generally in the salt works. A few became bushwhackers, outlaws who lived in the woods to escape conscription. As the drive for men for the Confederate army increased, they were hunted down and their families tortured until they gave information about the whereabouts of the missing members. Some were drafted and endured a great deal of disciplinary punishment from officers determined to make them bear arms. Several were strung up by their thumbs, or "bucked down," that is, tied head to heels, and kept in this position for many hours. Several died in army camps or army prison as a result of their sufferings.

Quaker families living in Virginia and North Carolina during the Civil War also endured a great deal, as first Confederate and then Union armies occupied their homes and requisitioned their food supplies. Many Quakers were imprisoned as potential Union sympathizers, and one man died of such imprisonment. After the war a primary concern of northern Friends was to relieve these sufferings and to restore the Society in the South. A Baltimore Association of Friends was formed for this purpose, and for many years raised money among Quakers everywhere to help rebuild the shattered southern meetings and nurse them back to health and vitality.

At the end of the war the work among the ex-slaves, or freedmen, became the great overriding concern of Quakers everywhere. In a sense, it was a time of release for Quakerdom. The deep compassion for the lot of the American Negro which had gripped the Society of Friends for almost two hundred years could now be expressed in the sort of practical relief and reconstruction work at which Quakers excel, without the political overtones inherent in the Underground Railroad movement. For once the Quakers were not confronting the government but cooperating with its effort to care for the ex-slaves. Responding to this challenge, many young Quakers flocked south to work among the freedmen, while their home meetings packed barrels of clothes, gathered tools, and raised money to support their enterprises.

All the various Quaker groups threw themselves enthusiastically into this work. Philadelphia Friends formed the Philadelphia Association for the Freedmen, which helped the Negroes plant gardens and build cabins on government grants of land, opened stores for the necessities of life, and established schools from Washington, D.C., down to North Carolina and Tennessee. By 1870 the Association managed forty-seven schools and sixty-seven teachers and six thousand students.

Friends of the New York Yearly Meeting began a similar project in 1862 and eventually built a system of industrial and elementary schools extending as far south as Tampa, Florida. New England Friends concentrated on schools and housing in the Washington, D.C., area. In 1875 they turned their schools over to Howard University and took charge of a training school for Negro teachers in Maryville, Tennessee. In 1865 Friends in Baltimore helped to form an association which developed a normal school, four industrial schools, and over seventy elementary schools for Negroes in Maryland.

In the Midwest, too, the Friends were active, the indomitable Levi Coffin helping to organize the Western Freedmen's Aid Commission which shipped clothing and other supplies to the ex-slaves grouped around Vicksburg and Little Rock. Schools and orphanges were established with the help of the Indiana Yearly Meeting's Committee on Contraband Relief.

As the immediate crisis lessened, and the public school systems became able to take over the freedmen's schools, the Friends began to concentrate on more specialized and permanent institutions, such as the normal schools in Baltimore and Tennessee, already mentioned, Southland College in Helena, Arkansas; the Industrial School at High Point, North Carolina; and a normal and industrial school at Aiken, North Carolina.

In 1879 there was a great migration of the freedmen into Kansas, about seventy thousand Negroes arriving in that state in a condition of great destitution. The Quakers who were already active in work with the ex-slaves responded to this new emergency and helped provide clothing, barracks, and schools, while they persuaded neighboring states to accept and find employment for large numbers of the refugees.

Typical of the Quaker work among the freedmen was that of Cornelia Hancock, a young Hicksite Quaker from Hancock Bridge, New Jersey. Cornelia became a Civil War nurse when scarcely twenty, served on several famous battlefields, and worked among the contraband outside of Washington. At the end of the war she went south to Charleston, South Carolina, and on the island of Mt. Pleasant began to work among the freedmen, distributing clothing and tools sent by the Hicksite Quakers of Philadelphia. She also started a small school in an abandoned Presbyterian Church, using charcoal from the remains of a fire to teach her first lesson.

From this beginning grew the Laing School which was operated by the Association of Friends for the Aid and Elevation of Freedmen and later by the Pennsylvania Abolition Society until 1938, when it finally became a public school. Graduates of Mt. Pleasant School still receive priority if they apply for scholarships through the Abolition Society, which continues to exist chiefly for the purpose of dispensing its revenues.

Cornelia Hancock herself stayed at the Laing School until 1876, then returned to Philadelphia. After a brief rest and a stimulating trip to England, she threw her energies into the problems of social work in that city. In 1878 she helped form a society which later became the Family Society of Philadelphia. In 1882 she helped form the Children's Aid of Pennsylvania. In 1884 she organized a startlingly modern self-help housing program in a poor section of Philadelphia called Wrightsville. At the end of her long life she clearly ranked as one of the great Quaker pioneers in social work.

# 7

# Pioneers in social change

Among Quakers there is no synonym for the word "concern." To have a concern means to have such compassion, to feel so keenly the plight of others, to care so much that one's duty is to take action. When a Quaker says, "I have a concern," he means that he is so troubled by the suffering of a person or a group of persons—the slaves, the American Indians, the prisoners, the mentally ill, the poor—that he feels a duty to act on their behalf.

Quakers feel that a true concern is divinely inspired. It is this faith that gives them the temerity—or the brass—to follow the concern wherever it may lead them. Mary Fisher felt a concern to visit the Sultan; John Woolman, to call upon the rich southern slaveholders and tell them to give up their property. During the Civil War several delegations of obscure Quakers went to Washington and persevered, until they managed to see President Lincoln, in order to share with him their concern that he liberate the slaves and stop the war. A concern led Quakers to go to the Gestapo after the Day of Broken Glass and ask for an end to the persecution of the Jews.

Although he may feel a concern deeply, a Quaker is never sure that it is divine until his meeting is in unity with him. He therefore shares his feelings with his meeting as urgently as possible. In the process he is likely to persuade the other members to feel as he does. This translation of individual sensitivity into group concern is one of the secrets of Quaker strength in the field of social action. With the support of the group behind him, the concerned individual is free to experiment with new ways of solving social problems.

One reason for Quaker sensitivity to suffering is the fact that Friends themselves were often poor, often imprisoned, and occasionally pushed to the verge of insanity during the early days of persecution. Another reason, many Quakers themselves believe, is the nature of the silent meeting for worship. Most people build mental walls against the troubles of others. Quakers do this too. But in the silent meeting ideas which have been pushed aside all week come bobbing up to disturb the individual's peace of mind. Many a Quaker concern has been born in the heart of a silent worshiper as he sits on a hard wooden bench and tries to open himself to the promptings of the Inner Light.

Whatever the reason, American Quakers have been on the growing edge of social change in many areas. Occasionally the name of an individual Quaker has remained in history as a

pioneer. More often, small groups of Quakers have been the
forerunners of social reforms which have come to fruition under
other leadership. To the concerned Friend what matters most
is getting the idea translated into action. This to him is the
Christian message. Someone once called the Quakers the most
practical mystics the world has ever seen.

### INDIANS

Throughout the colonial period Quakers tried to be just in their
dealings with the various tribes of American Indians and to influence the colonial governments to do likewise. Shortly after the
Revolutionary War it became evident to Friends that they must
also serve the Indians as friends at court. Under the pressure of
migrating frontiersmen the United States Government seemed
determined to take away from the Indians all the lands east of
the Mississippi. The Indians had an entirely different concept of
the ownership of land than the white man, and could hardly
understand what was happening to them. Bewildered, they
turned to the Quakers for help.

In 1793 two Indian messengers came all the way from the
Northwest Territory to Philadelphia to request that some Quakers
attend a council at Detroit between the United States Government and the Six Nations. In response, the Meeting for Sufferings
sent a delegation of six. Though little progress was made at this
gathering toward a settlement, it gave the Quakers a chance to
get to know many of the Indians. Next year, when the government called for another conference, this time at Canandaigua, the
Indians once more requested Quaker help. Four men, William
Savery, David Bacon, John Parrish, and James Emlen were
sent by the Philadelphia Friends.

At Canandaigua a solemn treaty was signed by the Sachems
of Six Nations and Timothy Pickering, United States Secretary of
State. The treaty itself seemed fair enough, though it was broken

many times thereafter. The Quaker delegation however was saddened by the general situation of the Indians and felt "under weighty concern" to do something to help them. On their return they reported to the Yearly Meeting:

> Many are the difficulties and sufferings to which the Indians are subject, and their present situation appears loudly to claim the sympathy and attention of the members of our religious Society and others who have grown opulent on the former inheritance of these poor declining people.

The following year Philadelphia Yearly Meeting decided to establish an Indian Affairs Committee. The first act of this group was to send three Quakers to live among the Oneidas on their reservation in New York in 1796. Their plan was to teach blacksmithing, animal husbandry, improved farm methods, and perhaps a little reading and writing. The New York Friends took this project over after several years, and the Philadelphia group transferred their efforts to the Allegheny reservation. Here they worked among the Senecas, first at Old Town and later at Tunesassa, teaching a number of related farm skills. In time they established a boarding school which operated continuously from 1852 to 1938.

The reawakened interest of the Philadelphia Friends in the Indians affected the other yearly meetings as well. New England Quakers began to help the Passamaquoddy and the Penobscot tribes in Maine with agriculture. New York Friends sent a man and wife to live among the Brotherton Indians, and kept in touch with the Oneida, the Onondaga, and the Stockbridge. Following the Hicksite-Orthodox separation in 1827, the New York Hicksite Friends established a center among the Senecas at Cattaraugus, and eventually set up a school.

The treaty of Canandaigua, signed by George Washington, and guaranteed—the Senecas thought—by the presence of Friends, was first threatened in 1809. A business outfit called the

Ogden Land Company obtained title to all the Seneca lands in New York State by bribing certain of the chiefs. When the Indians realized what had happened they came, in their distress, to the Quakers. The Friends in turn gathered the facts about the case and presented them to President Van Buren and to the Senate. The President was impressed, but the Senate went ahead anyway and ratified the treaty with the fraudulent chiefs. Although the Quakers tend to be shy of publicity, in this situation they felt they had to arouse public opinion against the shady deal. Their pamphleteering and speechmaking succeeded, and in 1842 they arranged a conference between the Secretary of War, the agents of the Ogden Land Company, and a group of representative Quakers. As a result, the Land Company got a portion of the tract but the Senecas retained the reservations at Cattaraugus and Allegheny.

Less than a hundred years later, the battle had to be fought all over again. In 1928, the United States Corps of Army Engineers recommended building a dam at Kinzua, Pennsylvania, to provide flood control of the Allegheny River. The result would be the flooding of the long, narrow, fertile Allegheny River valley, much of it Seneca tribal land. The Indians objected to the breaking of their treaty and fought the project vigorously, once more enlisting the help of the Sons of Onas. Dr. Arthur E. Morgan, a Quaker and once head of the Tennessee Valley Authority, was hired to survey the area. After a great deal of study he came up with a plan which would leave the Allegheny reservation untouched while providing, he claimed, superior flood control and storage facilities on another tributary. Such a dam would have to be built in addition to Kinzua in another twenty-five years anyway, Morgan insisted, therefore why not build it now and spare the Indian lands?

This alternative plan was not adopted; and, despite a vigorous program of public protest, the appropriation bill was finally passed by Congress in 1961. Friends next devoted themselves to pushing for legislation that would provide for the adequate compensation and resettlement for the Senecas. Such a bill was finally passed, but the Indians felt, understandably, that no compensation could make up for their lost homelands, or the breaking of a treaty. They moved off with bitter hearts.

As the Quakers migrated west during the nineteenth century, they took their concern for the Indians with them. In 1804 a small Quaker mission was established among the Indians near Fort Wayne, Indiana. Later the newly formed Ohio Yearly Meeting organized a school for the Shawnee Indians at Wapakoneta, Ohio. After some years this tribe moved west to Kansas. As they left, they bid their Quaker friends an affectionate farewell.

"We have been brothers together with you for a long time. You took us by the hand and held us fast. We have held you fast too. And although we are going far away from you, we do not want you to forsake us."

The Broadbrims, as the Indians sometimes called the Quakers, did not forsake the Shawnee. As soon as the tribe was settled in Kansas, representatives of Indiana Yearly Meeting came to see how the Indians were getting along in their new home. As a result of this visit the Yearly Meeting opened a school in 1837 and operated it until 1869. Quakers from all the major Orthodox meetings in America, as well as from Ireland and England, joined in supporting this enterprise. Boys learned to farm as well as to read and write, while girls were taught to knit and sew. Though disturbed several times by border raiders during the Free Soil controversy, the school managed to survive the stormy days of the Civil War. It finally closed because the Indians had moved farther west and there were not enough pupils left to make this operation worthwhile.

Throughout these years the Quakers continued to represent

the Indians in Washington. They regularly presented Congress with the memorials prepared by the various yearly meetings calling for more just treatment of the tribes. They also undertook specific commissions. One of the most persistent Quaker lobbyists was Thomas Wistar, II. His father had been a member of the first Indian Committee of Philadelphia Yearly Meeting, and he himself was active for many years in the work of the Associated Executive Committee of Friends on Indian Affairs, organized to coordinate the Indian work of nine yearly meetings. He traveled frequently and far, visiting Indians on their reservations from New York to the West. The conditions he found moved him so deeply that the Indians called him "the-man-with-a-tear-in-his-eye." In 1849 he was sent by the United States Government as a special commissioner to distribute $40,000 among the Menominees at Green Bay, Wisconsin, and in 1865 and 1866 he was appointed as a member of a special government commission to treat with the western Indian tribes.

In recognition of the good feeling developed between Friends and Indians by men such as Thomas Wistar, President Ulysses S. Grant decided to embark upon an experiment at the end of the Civil War. Since the Quakers and the Indians had lived at peace for so many years, why not ask the Quakers to help make peace with the midwestern tribes made uneasy and hostile by the arrival of more and more white settlers? In February, 1869, he asked both the Orthodox and the Hicksite branches if they would be willing to undertake the administration of several superintendencies of Indian reservations and to appoint Quaker Indian agents throughout these territories.

After a period of deliberation both bodies of Quakers agreed. The Orthodox would take the Central Superintendency, embracing Kansas; while the Hicksites would be responsible for the Northern Superintendency, including Nebraska. Quakers were appointed as superintendents in both regions, and Quaker agents were chosen to serve under them. The whole matter was accomplished so quickly that by December of 1869 Grant was able to announce the new policy to Congress in his first annual message:

> I have attempted a new policy toward these wards of the nation. . . . The Society of Friends is well known to have succeeded in living at peace with the Indians in the early settlement of Pennsylvania, while their white neighbors of other sects in other sections were constantly embroiled. They are also known for their opposition to all strife, violence, and war, and are generally noted for their strict integrity and fair dealings. These considerations induced me to give the management of a few reservations of Indians to them and to throw the burden of the selection of agents upon the Society itself. The results have proved most satisfactory.

Later, Grant appointed other religious denominations to manage other areas. This policy was continued for ten years, until Rutherford B. Hayes became President. The latter appointed a new Commissioner of Indian Affairs who was apparently hostile to the plan, and the Quakers soon found it necessary to resign their official positions.

During the ten years, however, much was accomplished. Aside from helping to settle many grievances peaceably, the Quakers established many new schools and agricultural stations. Many Friends came to work in these institutions during the era of Quaker management, and some remained in the Indian Service long after superintendencies were turned back to the government.

As the federal government took over more and more of the Indian schools, the Friends turned their efforts to the administration of more specialized institutions for higher education. This paralleled the development of their work in the South for the freedmen, at about the same period. In 1850 Philadelphia

Quaker Josiah White died, leaving a legacy for the establishment of schools in Iowa and Indiana. White's Institutes served as boarding schools for promising Indian students. At about the same time a boarding school was established for the eastern branch of the Cherokee Nation in Cherokee, North Carolina.

Throughout the early years of the nineteenth century the Quakers had taught the Indians scriptures along with reading and writing, but had put on no particular drive to convert them. In the 1880's and 1890's, however, the midwestern Friends, having been through a period of religious revival, became interested in purely religious work among the Indians. They established religious missions throughout the Oklahoma Territory and later in Alaska, converted many Indians and developed several local meetings. It was during this period that such colorful names as Scar-Faced Charlie, Birdie Spoon, Aunt Mary Bourbonnais, and Thomas Wildcat Alford were added to the lists of members of the Society of Friends.

By the early 1920's both eastern and midwestern Friends were interested in coupling religious instruction with a practical form of community and social work. Shortly after the conclusion of World War I, a number of young Friends went to live and work on the Indian lands in Oklahoma, helping with recreation, farming, and the redevelopment of such crafts as weaving, pottery, and basket making. A new respect for Indian culture and an effort to revitalize it marked the approach of these younger Friends.

In 1929 President Herbert Hoover, himself a Quaker, appointed two Philadelphia Quakers as Commissioners of Indian Affairs. During their four-year terms they overhauled the Indian Service, and improved the schools, health services, and agricultural methods. Young Indians leaving the reservations were given help in counseling and job placement during this period. For the first time a conscious effort was made to help the Indians take pride in their heritage.

Throughout the Depression years various Quaker groups kept in close touch with Indian problems. The American Friends Service Committee, by then a going concern, organized summer work camps on Indian reservations in which young men and women of high school and college age worked alongside the Indians in community self-help projects. In 1947 the AFSC undertook emergency relief work among the Navajos after a severe drought that brought them close to starvation.

From this beginning the AFSC developed a national Indian program. In parts of California, Arizona, and Montana, workers lived on reservations with the Indians, sharing their life and encouraging them to undertake self-help projects of the sort that develop leadership and a sense of dignity. In Oakland, California, an Inter-tribal Friendship House, run by the AFSC, assists off-reservation Indians to maintain a feeling of identity as they adjust to urban life.

With other organizations interested in Indian rights, the AFSC has opposed United States Government efforts to implement a termination policy to which the Indians object. Treaty rights should not be brought to an abrupt end, Quakers say, until the Indians are in accord, and until there are means for providing enough services and compensation to help the Indians make a gradual transition. During 1968 Quakers defended the rights of a group of Indians in the Northwest—Nisqually, Puyallup, Muckleshoot, and Yakima tribes—to fish without restriction in the game-rich rivers of the former Oregon Territory. Such fishing rights were given to the Indians by treaty but were disputed by the state of Oregon's game wardens under pressure from the sportsmen's organizations. The Indians staged a series of "fish-ins" to bring their plight to the attention of the public, and the Quakers helped them to make a study of the legal rights of their situation.

## PRISONS

It is very hard for us today to imagine the conditions in the prisons of the seventeenth century. Many consisted of one large room into which all the prisoners were herded together, male or female, sick or well, old or young, condemned murderer or young thief. If they had any money the convicts could occasionally secure separate quarters or at least provide themselves with food. Otherwise they were reduced to begging out of the windows to the passerby for crusts of bread. People who were in debt were thrown into prisons, illogically enough, until the debt was paid. The punishment for crime generally consisted of beating, mutilating, or beheading. Over two hundred crimes were punishable by death.

Since the Quakers could not, as a matter of conscience, pay the jailers any special fees for special privileges, they endured the very worst of these conditions along with thieves and murderers. Many died in prison in the early years. It was out of the depth of this personal involvement that Quakers first felt the driving compassion for prisoners which has been one of their distinguishing characteristics.

In 1650, when he was a prisoner in Derby, George Fox wrote to the judge on the subject "concerning their putting men to death for (stealing) cattle and money and small matters. I laid it before the judges," he said, "what a hurtful thing it was that the prisoners lie so long in jail, showing how they learned badness one of another in talking about their deeds, and therefore speedy justice should be done."

Having himself spent time in the Tower of London, William

Penn was eager to include penal reform in his Holy Experiment. In Pennsylvania's Frame of Government, the two hundred capital offenses were cut to two, murder and treason. As a Quaker Penn would have liked to abolish capital punishment entirely, but this was not possible under the charter he held from the King. All prisons, according to Penn, were to provide free food and lodging, and to serve as work houses, providing useful employment for "felons, vagrants, and loose and idle persons." Penn's prisons were regarded as model institutions throughout the colonies, but after his death they lapsed considerably.

In 1787 an association called the Philadelphia Society for Alleviating the Miseries of the Public Prisons was established in Philadelphia. Benjamin Franklin, Dr. Benjamin Rush, and a group of freethinkers were present at the first meeting, along with many Quakers. The Society has continued ever since as an ecumenical affair with a strong Quaker influence. Its first project was to convert the Walnut Street Jail into an experimental institution. The group wanted to try out a new idea. Instead of merely being confined, prisoners were to be given an opportunity to meditate about their past sins and resolve to live a better life. To this end the prison was planned to provide separate, or solitary, confinement for the prisoners. Meditation and moral instruction, both Quaker concepts, were to be used instead of the brutal punishments of the day. The new jail was called a penitentiary, a place where the prisoners could do penance.

As against the old concepts of death, torture, and dismemberment as the way to deal with crime, the idea of separate confinement was an improvement. For the first time society acknowledged that even the most hardened criminal might be reformed. In Quaker terms, it meant recognition that there is that of God in every man. Though Friends and their friends could not foresee it, however, solitary confinement became a form of torture to many prisoners, breaking their spirit and driving them to the verge of insanity.

In 1829 Eastern Penitentiary, a new institution built according to the "Pennsylvania System" of separate confinement, was ready to receive its first inmates. Individual cells, each with its small exercise yard, were provided for each prisoner. Prisoners were hooded upon entry into the prison, and throughout their stay the utmost effort was made to keep them from so much as seeing a fellow prisoner. During religious services the heavy solid door to each cell was opened, but a thick net was hung over the bars, thus preventing the prisoners from seeing each other while they listened to a common service from a pastor in the corridor.

In theory, the prison's solitude was to be broken by visits from members of the Philadelphia Society, by friendly wardens, by prison officials bringing the prisoners a certain amount of piece work—shoe cobbling or weaving for example—to keep them occupied. In practice the prisoner was virtually isolated from all human contact. Visiting Eastern Penitentiary in 1842, Charles Dickens was so appalled by the awful effects of isolation that he wrote a scathing account of it in his *American Notes for General Circulation:*

> It seems to me the objection that nothing wholesome or good has ever had its growth in such unnatural solitude . . . would be of itself a sufficient argument against the system. But when we recollect in addition how very cruel and severe it is and that a solitary life is always liable to peculiar and distinct objections of a most deplorable nature, which have arisen here . . . there is surely more than sufficient reason for abandoning a mode of punishment attended by so little hope or promise, and fraught, beyond dispute, with such a host of evils.

Members of the Philadelphia Society vehemently denied these charges and accused Dickens of allowing his fertile imagination to run away with him in the lurid descriptions of the prisoners. Nevertheless, the Pennsylvania System gradually became less popular, and was finally abandoned, by 1900. Instead, a compromise was developed, under which prisoners worked and studied and worshiped together during the day, but were confined to separate quarters at night.

In New York State, meanwhile, prison reform had been advanced by the Friends under the leadership of a remarkable man. Thomas Eddy was a prominent Quaker businessman, one of the planners of the Erie Canal, and a pioneer in life insurance. He became comfortable financially rather early in life and devoted himself to a wide range of Quaker philanthropic interests. He represented New York Friends in their work with the Indians, helped to establish the Public School Society of New York, and struggled to create Bloomingdale, the state's first mental hospital. He became interested in the Pennsylvania system of separate confinement but felt it ought to be modified. Prisoners should be kept in separate cells at night, but allowed to work together, though in silence, in the course of the day. He was instrumental in the building of the first state prison in New York City, and later, the first state penitentiary at Auburn, where many of his ideas were applied.

The involvement of Quakers in prison reform on both sides of the Atlantic was given impetus in 1813 when a charming Quaker woman began to visit the female prisoners of Newgate in London. Elizabeth Fry was a member of the rich and popular Gurney family of Earlham Hall, a sister to Joseph John Gurney, the minister. As a girl she had been as worldly as her brothers and sisters, enjoying gay clothes and finding the local Friends Meeting "disgusting." At seventeen, however, she was deeply touched by the preaching of William Savery, a Philadelphia Quaker, and from then on became increasingly Quakerly in her tastes and interests. In 1800 she married Joseph Fry, a banker, and thereafter divided her time between good works and her large family of eleven children.

It was Stephen Grellet, another American Quaker, who introduced Elizabeth Fry to the conditions at Newgate. Appalled by the misery, overcrowding, and vice, she got immediately to work, persuading the prison authorities to permit her to conduct a sewing workshop for the female inmates and organizing a society of public spirited citizens to help with the improvement of prison conditions. Eventually she was able to bring the situation of prisoners to public attention, and to help achieve widespread reforms.

Inspired by Elizabeth Fry, a group of women Friends in Philadelphia founded one of the early halfway houses in the United States, Howard Institution. Located in a house on Poplar Street, it was opened in 1853 and received discharged prisoners until 1907, when it became a home for delinquent girls. At first the Pennsylvania Prison Society (as the Philadelphia Society was renamed) did not support Howard, since it violated their basic philosophy by allowing discharged prisoners to mingle and so contaminate each other. Eventually, however, they relented and helped the ladies support the institution.

Throughout all these years the Quakers visited prisons and kept in close contact with the condition of the prisoners. One of the outstanding Friendly visitors was Isaac Hopper, the peppery little Napoleon of the Underground Railroad. Isaac was an inspector for the Philadelphia prison, and became in time nearly as famous for espousing the cause of prisoners as of escaped slaves. He was especially concerned about the young prisoners who were thrown in with hardened criminals.

One day when Hopper was visiting the penitentiary two boys in their teens arrived handcuffed together. They had been sentenced to two years at hard labor for giving false evidence against the character of a neighbor in Carlisle, Pennsylvania. Investigating, Hopper learned that they had lied at the insistence of their father, an irrational and vindictive person. He took an interest in their case, visited them regularly in prison, and when the Board of Inspectors next met, recommended them for a pardon. Overruled in this, he wrote an article for the leading papers in which he criticized the policy of mixing juveniles with older criminals. Public opinion swung to his side, and when the Board of Inspectors next met he won his point. Hopper then found men who were willing to accept the two boys as apprentices and continued his interest in them until they were safely married and settled with their families.

After he moved to New York, Isaac Hopper became an agent for the Prison Association of that city. Both during and after working hours he visited prisons, helped discharged prisoners readjust, and worked to improve prison conditions. Until the end of his long life he visited Albany regularly, applying for pardons from the governor, and working for prison reforms. In 1845 the Female Department of the New York Prison Association, under the leadership of a daughter, Abby Hopper Gibbons, founded the first halfway house for women prisoners in the world. Today the Isaac Hopper Home in New York continues to serve as a haven for recently paroled women and girls.

Though Hopper was exceptionally active, other Friends during this period, led either by individual concern, membership in a prison society, or by the concern of their monthly meetings, visited prisoners regularly. These Friends helped to develop prison associations in other states, under the leadership of the Pennsylvania Society. Their firsthand knowledge of the condition of prisons and prisoners caused Quakers to press for prison reform on both a local and a national basis.

Firsthand knowledge came also as a result of personal involvement. By 1775 Quakers were no longer being thrown into prison for refusal to pay tithing fees, but during both the Revolutionary War and the Civil War they were given jail sentences for nonpayment of war taxes, and for refusal to serve in the army. Although conscientious objectors were legally recognized by the draft law in World War I, their disposition was left in the hands of military officers often unacquainted with the CO provisions. As a result many CO's wound up in army stockades, and some endured maltreatment at the hands of officers eager to turn them into "men." During World War II the CO's were placed under civilian control, but many young men objected to the narrow limits of the options open to them, and to the draft system itself. These absolutists, some two thousand of them, served terms in federal penitentiaries where they were treated like common prisoners. Like their spiritual ancestors some three hundred years ago, they objected to the conditions of this treatment not for themselves but for their fellow prisoners

During World War II many Quaker meetings revived the practice of prison visiting to keep in touch with the conscientious objectors. After the war ended and the CO's left, the volunteers stayed with the job, visiting more conventional prisoners. In the California area this program in turn led to the creation by the Quakers of halfway houses: Crenshaw House in Los Angeles which opened in 1958, and Elizabeth Fry House in 1966. In San Francisco and in Des Moines, Iowa, similar homes are in operation. They serve as a welcoming base for prisoners just released from prison and not yet quite ready to be on their own in the community.

Throughout their three-hundred-year history Quakers have been opposed to the death penalty. One cannot believe in reformation while destroying the potential reformee. To be in favor of the abolition of capital punishment is a natural extension of the Quaker testimony that violence is the wrong way to achieve any goals. The Friends cite statistics which show that neither in nations nor in the states where capital punishment has been abandoned has there been a significant increase in crime. Through their Washington legislative wing, the Friends Committee on National Legislation, the Quakers continually seek to outlaw capital punishment nationally.

## THE MENTALLY ILL

The early persecution, which placed thousands of Quakers in jail and acquainted them firsthand with the condition of prisoners, also drove a few Friends to the verge of insanity. Whether this personal factor influenced them or not, Quakers were among the first to call for humane treatment for the mentally ill. In 1669 George Fox advised his followers to provide "a house for them that be distempered." This was, for his day, a brand-new idea. The mentally ill were treated on the supposition that they were possessed of demons. They were punished, baited, and made sport of. In the infamous hospital at Bethlehem—"Bedlam"—patients were exhibited for the amusement of the public as late as 1770.

Even before Fox's urging, one Quaker physician, Dr. John Goodson, had opened his home "for distempered and discomposed persons." Evidently he made there the first experimental attempt to deal with patients without mechanical restraints. This experiment was ended when Goodson emigrated to Philadelphia. There he may have been one of the Quakers to nurse along the idea of establishing some sort of hospital to provide care for the mentally ill. At any rate such a group was developed, and by the mid-eighteenth century was successful in enlisting the enthusiasm of Benjamin Franklin and other prominent non-Friends in their project. When Pennsylvania Hospital opened its doors in 1751 it was the first hospital in the world to offer medical care for the insane.

That care was, to be sure, fairly crude. The patients were kept in the cellar and subjected to a medical treatment that sounds barbarous today. Their scalps were shaved and blistered, they were bled almost to death, given enemas until they were faint, and chained by waist or ankle to the cell walls, or fastened up in a "madd-shirt" or straitjacket. Still, the idea was cure, not punishment, however brutal the methods. In addition, the patients were given flax and wool with which to spin. This was the first use of occupational therapy with the mentally ill.

While this was being attempted in the New World, an equal concern in England led to the establishment in 1796 of York Retreat, an institution designed specifically and solely for the care of the mental patients. William Tuke, its founder, was determined to try Quaker principles in its administration and to use dignity, even tenderness, rather than restraints on the disturbed patients. Men and women who had been chained behind bars were able for the first time in years to sleep in beds and sit at tables under this gentle treatment. If York Retreat did not immediately return patients to sanity, it made their shadowed days far more livable.

In 1799 Thomas Scattergood, a Philadelphia Quaker, visited the York Retreat. Scattergood was a Quaker minister of the old school. A Quietist, he refused to speak in meeting, or make a decision of any nature, unless he felt himself to be under divine guidance. On one of his missionary trips to western Pennsylvania he sat through seven successive meetings for worship, his tears falling upon his folded hands, because he could not speak. Though many had come from miles around to hear him he felt "closed to public communication." He went to England in 1794 under "a leading of the spirit" and stayed for eight years, often homesick but convinced that this was what God wanted of him. In point of fact, the trip proved a very useful one. While in England he learned from the English Friends about the Lancaster schools for poor children. Under the Lancaster method, the older pupils tutored the younger ones, so that many could be educated for very little. Returning to Philadelphia he helped to establish a public school for Negro children based on this method.

Seven months after Thomas Scattergood first visited York he "felt a concern to go to the retreat, a place where about thirty of our society are taken in being disordered of mind. We got most of them together, and after we had sat a little in quiet, and I had vented a few tears, I was engaged in supplication." He prayed for the inmates, and felt a response in their tenderness and gratitude. The experience so moved him that he became determined to establish a similar institution in the United States.

Fourteen years later, in 1813, Frankford Asylum just outside of Philadelphia opened its doors. It was the first private mental hospital in the United States. According to its constitution it was "intended to furnish, beside the requisite medical aid, such tender sympathetic attention and religious oversight as may soothe their agitated minds and thereby, under the divine blessing, facilitate their restoration to the enjoyment of this inestimable gift."

Friends Hospital, as it is now called, operated from the first on the principles of "occupation" and "nonrestraint." The annual report of 1853 claims it was the first hospital in the United States where a chain was never used for the confinement of a patient. Instead, all the inmates who were able worked on the grounds or in the sewing rooms, played tennis or croquet, attended teas and lectures, or took rides through the park that surrounds the hospital. All these practices, standard today in a good private mental hospital, were revolutionary in the early nineteenth century. Today Friends Hospital continues to be known as a place where patients can enjoy a maximum of personal dignity while being confined.

Another Quaker to be influenced by the York Retreat was Thomas Eddy. After reading a book by William Tuke's grandson, Samuel Tuke, describing the Retreat, Eddy presented the New York Hospital Board, of which he was a member, with a plan for the "moral management of the insane." As a result Blooming-dale Asylum was opened in 1818. This hospital was a model for its day and became the predecessor of the Westchester Division of the New York Hospital in White Plains.

In 1841, Pennsylvania Hospital opened an institution for the care of the insane in West Philadelphia with Dr. Thomas Kirkbride, a Quaker, as its first superintendent. Dr. Kirkbride had served as a resident physician at Friends Hospital in Frankford, and was eager to try the experiment of using "moral suasion" rather than mechanical restraint at the new Pennsylvania Institute. In fact, he succeeded. During one ten-day period the new hospital was run without any use of restraint for its one hundred patients. For those times it was a record. Dr. Kirkbride is remembered also as the founder of "the Association of Medical Superintendents of American Institutions for the Insane," the parent body to the present American Psychiatric Association.

Through institutions such as Friends Hospital, Quakers kept alive their concern for mental illness through the years, and a few Quakers entered the field of psychiatry. During World War II many conscientious objectors were assigned to work as ward attendants in state mental hospitals as an alternative to military service. The overcrowding and understaffing, the consequent filth and neglect in many of these institutions at the time, was shocking to the young CO's. In some hospitals there was only one doctor to a thousand patients. On occasion a patient who had died remained in the ward for several days until he could be seen by a doctor and pronounced dead. Except for electroshock therapy, used for the most violent patients, there was little that could be described as treatment.

The CO's did not keep quiet about this situation. There were headlines in many local newspapers, and several congressional investigations followed the revelations. In the Quaker unit in the State Hospital at Byberry, Pennsylvania, four young men organized a national association through which the attendants could call for reform in mental hospitals. This was a forerunner of the National Association for Mental Health, an organization which has done much in the past years to bring public attention to the problems of mental illness.

When the CO's took over the management of a ward in a mental hospital, a remarkable change often took place. Violence, even on the violent ward, decreased, locked cells were opened, straitjackets put away. Even the most disturbed patients, it was discovered, reacted to the quiet, the courtesy, and the absence of fear on the part of their new attendants.

Recognizing these positive reactions, hospital superintendents asked for more CO units. When there were not enough conscientious objectors to fill the need, young wives and sweethearts were recruited to serve in women's units. Even after World War II ended, this program continued. For the past twenty years the American Friends Service Committee has recruited young college and high school men and women to work in mental hospitals, training schools, and correctional institutions during the summers, and sometimes for weekends during the year.

## POVERTY AND EQUAL RIGHTS

Many of the early Quakers were drawn from a class suffering the effects of depression in the middle of the seventeenth century. Persecution and imprisonment added to the impoverishment of their families. During its first fifty years the Society of Friends in England and in the United States was hard pressed to take care of its own poor. It was for this purpose that Meetings for Sufferings, as they were called, were organized, and that the method of registering Quakers as "birthright" was evolved.

Nevertheless the early Quakers felt a lively compassion for other poor people, and a few members of the Society began to try to think of remedies to poverty in general. One of these was John Bellers, a wealthy cloth merchant. In 1695 Bellers published "Proposals for a College of Industry." In this he suggested the establishment of working communities where men and women could practice a variety of trades, children could be educated, and young people apprenticed.

In 1701 this visionary scheme was tried out on a small scale. The London Friends, urged on by Bellers, took over a work-house in Clerkenwell and formed it into a small model "college." For several years it worked according to plan, but was never very successful in holding men and women in the middle years. Instead, it gradually became a school and an old people's home combined. In time, the old people's home dwindled away, and the school metamorphosed into an institution for the children of the Friends, rather than the poor. Today it is an excellent Friends coeducational boarding and day school at Saffron Walden, in Essex.

Bellers had many other ideas for social reform and for the achievement of peace through world government. Coming across his writings 150 years later, Karl Marx described him as a "veritable phenomenon in the history of political economy." Today Bellers is more widely known and read in the communist countries than in Great Britain or the United States. His kind of overall deductive approach to social change has been rare in the history of Quaker thought. Friends generally work inductively, following a particular concern in a particular situation. They proceed, according to a pithy Quaker saying, as way opens. Only when the particular leads them to a feeling for the desirability of widespread social change do they work for social reform on a broad scale.

In colonial America, as well, the Quakers first took care of their own poor, then, as they became a little more affluent, concerned themselves with the establishment of almshouses and schools for the poor in general. Following the American Revolution they became increasingly concerned for those whose poverty resulted from discrimination, primarily the slaves and the Indians. The establishment of elementary schools, then trade and agricultural schools for both the Indians and the freedmen took up much of the time and energy of the Society during the nineteenth century.

In the latter part of that century new minorities began to appear in the heart of the American cities as wave after wave of European immigration brought Italians and Germans, Poles and Irish, Russians and Lithuanians to this country. Quakers were active in the settlement house movement which grew up to meet the needs of these new citizens. In Chicago, Jane Addams, the daughter of a self-styled Hicksite Quaker, founded the famous Hull House on Halstead Street. Though never herself a Quaker, Jane Addams was always close to Friends, and later worked in Europe for the American Friends Service Committee. In Philadelphia, Quakers helped to develop a mission on Water Street which later became Friends Neighborhood Guild, a settlement house that has pioneered in self-help housing and other forms of neighborhood rehabilitation.

During these decades American Quakers also were busy with another crusade: the temperance movement. Before this time Quakers had stressed the idea of temperance and moderation as a goal for themselves and others. Now however they began to feel that alcoholic beverages had such an evil effect on the people whom they were trying to help—the Indians on the reservation, the slum dwellers in the big cities—that it would be best if no one drank at all, and thus avoided leading others into temptation. The revivalist movement that swept the American frontier in the 1860's was closely linked with the idea of pledging total abstinence. Although only a part of Quakerism became involved in the evangelical revivals, the whole Society of Friends in America took up the Temperance Movement.

Women's rights became an issue at about the same time as the abolition of slavery. The two causes had a common moral base: a person's right to be treated as a human being worthy of dignity regardless of race or sex. Quakers had believed in this right from the beginning and had treated women as equal in the home, the schoolroom and the meetinghouse long before the rest of society caught up. Most Quaker boarding schools and colleges, established in the course of the nineteenth century, were open to both boys and girls from the start. As early as 1825 a Quaker educator was writing, "There does not appear any reason why the education of women should differ in its essentials from that of men."

Quaker women who became involved in the women's rights movement were not known for wearing bloomers—though a few did—or advocating free love. Instead, most of the Quaker suffragists seemed cut from the same model as Lucretia Mott and Elizabeth Fry. They remained feminine and modest, calm and unruffled, while working wholeheartedly for the rights of their fellow human beings. Many Quaker women have been gifted at running large households serenely while attending to social reforms. The suffragists followed in that tradition. Perhaps this trait comes from the Quaker concept of simplicity.

Throughout the 1890's and the early 1900's Quakers continued to work on a group of related concerns; schools for Negroes and for Indians, women's rights, temperance, prison reform, and the assimilation of new Americans. They established day nurseries and homes for working girls, reflecting a growing concern with the place of women in an increasingly industrial society. Nevertheless, like most Americans, Quakers in these decades shared an optimistic belief that most social problems could be solved, given a measure of goodwill, and a strong effort on the part of the poor to better their own situation. Social concerns, though pressing, did not grip the Society of Friends generally with the force that became driving in the twentieth century.

World War I was a time of awakening from the dreams of inevitable progress. It was also, for the American Quakers, a time of challenge. Deeply opposed to the war, they found they had become too sophisticated to explain and justify this opposition in the simple terms of their forefathers. They could no longer be simply *against* the use of violence, they must be *for* a society which was nonviolently ordered throughout its structure. They needed, in the terms of William James, to find a moral equivalent to war.

The American Friends Service Committee was founded in 1917 by a group of representatives of all branches of Quakerism. Its purpose was to provide the Society in general, and its young conscientious objectors in particular, an opportunity to perform what its founders called "a service of love in wartime." Choosing as its symbol a red-and-black star, it sent hundreds of young American men and women first to France, later to Germany, Russia, Poland, Serbia, Hungary, and Austria to give relief to war sufferers and to help in the job of reconstruction.

Other Quakers, too young to take part in this exciting adventure, began petitioning the newly formed Service Committee for comparable service opportunities within the United States.

In response the AFSC found work for them on Indian reservations, in settlement houses, in Negro schools in the South, in depressed areas of Appalachia. The failure of the bituminous coal industry in the 1920's brought unemployment to large areas of western Pennsylvania, West Virginia, and parts of Maryland, Kentucky, and Illinois. The Quaker volunteers were increasingly assigned to this region. Twice, in 1922 and 1928, the AFSC undertook emergency feeding of children of coal miners. In 1931 they were asked by President Herbert Hoover to feed hungry children throughout this area for an extended period of time.

Work in the coal fields, thus begun, became a major project for the American Quakers during the 1930's. Once the immediate crisis of widespread undernourishment was over, the Quakers stayed on to help with more long-term needs. A health service and family-planning clinic were established, recreational and adult education programs developed, and a furniture-making cooperative set up as a way of giving the unemployed miners some means of earning money. Later the Quakers played a part in the homesteading program of the New Deal, assisting communities to establish schools and community halls. During this period Eleanor Roosevelt, the wife of the President, gave all the money she earned by radio talks to the Quakers to be spent in the coal fields.

In 1937 the AFSC purchased six hundred acres for the creation of a model homestead community, Penncraft, in western Pennsylvania. Here each family was loaned money with which to build their own home. Families then took turns helping to erect each house in the community, and various of the men involved developed differing specialities. The pattern of self-help housing which was developed in this fashion was a new and useful idea in community development. Later, the Quakers helped to launch self-help co-op projects in a slum section of Philadelphia, among Mexican-American migrant workers in California, among rural farmworkers in New Jersey and Pennsylvania, and in a depressed section of Indianapolis.

World War II brought a period of full employment to the coal fields, as well as other depressed areas, and the AFSC was gradually able to end its work in Appalachia. Instead, there were soon many new problems to face. The war industries drew many southern Negroes to northern and western cities. Patterns of discrimination in housing, schools, and jobs, which had been there all along, suddenly became glaringly evident under the pressure of this in-migration. The Quakers, again through the AFSC, responded by working first in the field of merit employment, persuading employers to hire on the basis of skill rather than race. A short time later they began also to organize citizens to work on fair housing, finding opportunities for Negro families to live in previously all-white neighborhoods in the cities and suburbs. They have also worked for school desegregation in both the North and the South.

Though the AFSC became, in the course of the twentieth century, the best known and the largest of the Quaker service organizations in the United States, it had no corner on Quaker concern. Both pastoral and evangelical Friends continued to work with the Indians. Monthly, quarterly, and yearly meetings sponsored volunteer work in prisons and mental hospitals. Groups of Friends in big cities became involved in providing meeting places and encouraging leadership among slum dwellers. Many individual Friends were engaged in some form of service —tutoring slum children, helping in the readjustment of mental patients, visiting prisoners.

The programs run by the Quakers are almost all very small. They can properly be regarded as pilot projects, experiments, which if successful can be turned over to community groups, to the government, or the schools for implementation. If they fail no great harm is done. This fact permits Quakers to experiment with new ideas for social change and keeps them in the pioneering frontier of social reform. Many of their projects, once unique, now have been taken up by other religious or humanitarian groups. Instead of continuing to operate programs that compete, the Quakers move on to fresh experiments.

# 8

# The Quaker contribution to the cultural life of America

## EDUCATION

To George Fox and his fellow Quakers, the Truth which they experienced in quiet meditation, and proclaimed to the world, was as real and concrete as the stones, the grass, the brook, the sky. Having found for themselves this reality in spite of, and not because of, the long-winded argumentative sermons of the day, they were deeply suspicious of "notions" and "airy knowl-edge." In the language of semantics, they believed that the object itself, not the symbol used to describe the object, was really real.

When he planned the first Quaker schools, George Fox looked for ways to transpose this inductive approach to edu-cation. He proposed that such schools teach "whatsoever things are civil and useful in creation." With William Penn he drew plans for a garden house. All kinds of plants were to be gathered so that the students could observe them firsthand, then begin to learn such abstract matters as their names and classifi-cations.

Though land was set aside for the construction of this school in Philadelphia, it was never built. Nevertheless, Penn continued to advocate a pragmatic approach in the schools established under his Charter, of which William Penn Charter established in 1689 was the first. His educational philosophy, echoed a century later by Quaker schoolman, Moses Brown of Rhode island, was startlingly like that of the progressive educators of the 1920's:

> We are in pain to make them scholars but not men, to talk rather than to know, which is true canting. The first thing ob-vious to children is what is sensible; and that we make no part of their rudiments. We press their memory too soon and puzzle, strain, and load them with words and rules to know grammar and rhetoric; and a strange tongue or two that it is ten to one, may never be useful to them, leaving their natural genius to mechanical, and physical or natural knowledge un-cultivated and neglected, which would be of exceeding use and pleasure through the whole course of their lives.

> To be sure languages are not to be despised or neglected. But things are still to be preferred. Children had rather be making of tools and instruments of play, shaping, drawing, and build-ing, than getting some rules of propriety by heart, and those

> also would follow with more judgment and less trouble and time. It were happy if we studied nature more in natural things, and acted according to nature whose rules are few, plain, and reasonable.

Through the years, Quaker schools have emphasized practical subjects, and have been especially known for science and math, rather than the arts. Laboratory periods, field trips, and practical work experience projects have been featured in most of these schools, from kindergarten through college. When Quakers established schools for the freed slaves or the Indians they stressed agricultural skills or trades.

This emphasis on the concrete had its negative aspects also. For many years Friends saw no need for higher education. It was not until after the Revolutionary War that they established the first Quaker academies, the equivalent of high schools. Haverford, the oldest Quaker college, dates back to 1833, almost two hundred years later than the establishment of Harvard. This reluctance to become involved in the founding of higher educational institutions may have cost the Quakers their place of preeminence in colonial America. It certainly cost them many young men and women whose thirst for knowledge, particularly in the arts and the humanities, led them beyond the Quaker fold.

Nevertheless, when the Friends finally got around to establishing schools, they were mainly very good schools. The first Quaker academy to be established was the Moses Brown School in Portsmouth, Rhode Island, in 1784, later transferred to Providence in 1819. Second came Nine-Partners in New York, started in 1796, now the Oakwood School in Poughkeepsie. Westtown, in Pennsylvania, was begun in 1799 and New Garden Boarding School, now Guilford College, in 1837. Throughout the nineteenth century such academies were opened throughout the East and the Midwest. They were boarding schools designed at first to train teachers for the Quaker elementary schools. They all provided education for both boys and girls, though they did not become coeducational until a later date. The most stable ones, those that endured to this day, were under the care of the yearly meetings in their areas.

The Quaker colleges, founded mainly during the nineteenth century, included Haverford, Swarthmore (Pennsylvania), Guilford (North Carolina), Wilmington (Ohio), Malone (Ohio), Earlham (Indiana), William Penn (Iowa), Friends University (Kansas), Whittier (California), and George Fox (Oregon). In addition, one college and two universities, Bryn Mawr, Johns Hopkins, and Cornell were founded by individual Quakers. Most of these schools have maintained a reputation for educational excellence, combined with a strong emphasis on scientific subjects and concern for humanitarian projects. Two schools for graduate study, Pendle Hill in Wallingford, Pennsylvania, and the Earlham School of Religion in Richmond, Indiana, provide opportunities for the study of Quaker history and religious beliefs.

In the early days of this country, the small schools established by the Quakers were often the only schools to serve a rural area. Naturally many non-Quakers sent their children to these schools. The Quakers accepted such scholars, and did not ask a fee if the family was poor. Later, however, the Friends began to fear the effects of having their children schooled with the offspring of the "world's people." From the time of the Revolutionary War onward the Quakers put increasing emphasis on what they called a religiously guarded education. They wanted to prepare their children to take part in the special and separate community into which the Society of Friends was slowly turning. And they wanted to spare the children from the dangers of contamination by ideas and influence outside the circle of Quakerism.

Some modern Quakers have questioned the wisdom of this guarded education of their ancestors. Was it contradictory, they asked, for parents who themselves had found the Truth "experimentally" to insist on teaching their children only the "right" ideas? Were they producing children who could function only within the confines of a special community? More important, were they right in developing a distrust of outsiders?

Such a sense of set-apartness was certainly a result of guarded Quaker education. A woman who was born in 1892 writes in her journal:

> I, as a Friend, knew only the children who went to Friends School and felt that the others were a little strange and maybe naughty. I did live in a narrow little world. I'm not sure whether it was a righteous feeling we had, or a shyness, but I knew distinctly that Friends were different from the "World."

On the other hand, this sense of difference probably helped Quakers to stand out against public opinion; in working for freedom for the slaves, in opposing war, in going to jail rather than violating their consciences. It also produced strong, well-integrated characters with few inner conflicts who lived serene and useful lives. Even today there is a serenity about the Quakers born and bred within the fold. Such Friends turn back to their early Quaker schooling with affection and nostalgia, and draw from the school community continuing support.

The drive to provide Quaker children with a guarded education affected the degree to which Quakers became involved with public schools. In many parts of the country, where the Quaker day schools and academies were the first schools for the entire community, these schools gradually became the public schools. In some cases the township or the state paid the salaries of the Quaker teachers and rented the Quaker school rooms during the transition.

In Quaker strongholds, however, particularly along the East Coast, the Quakers continued to operate their separate schools, while encouraging the development of public schools for the rest of the population. Often the Quakers actually pioneered in the public school movement. In New York City some women Friends in 1801 organized schools for the education of poor children who were without religious affiliation. A few years later Thomas Eddy and other Friends helped to found the Public School Society. This group eventually took over the management of the schools organized by the Quaker women, the first Quaker school becoming New York City's P.S. One. Elsewhere Quakers helped to press for the establishment of public schools and sometimes served on school boards. An unusually high percentage of modern Quakers are teachers, many of them in the public schools.

Today the Quaker private schools continue to flourish in such cities as Washington, Baltimore, Philadelphia, New York, and Boston and their environs. Many non-Quakers send their children to these schools because of their reputation for academic excellence, attention to the needs of the individual, and services to the community. Though all students are required to attend Quaker meeting, and courses in Quaker history are taught as part of American history, no attempt is made to convert the non-Quaker students. An informal education in Quaker testimonies is provided implicitly by such practices as the exchange of foreign students, a racially mixed student body, notices on the bulletin boards announcing weekend work camps or institutional service units, recruitment among the student body for summer service projects.

Henry Seidel Canby, one of America's foremost men of

letters, was a non-Friend who attended the Quaker school in Wilmington, Delaware, in the 1890's. Of this experience he wrote:

> Under their [the Quakers'] gentle but powerful influence we acquired an instinct which subtly pervaded our later thinking. We found it difficult not to believe in the permanent possibility of good in any man. The naive (and yet not so naive either) faith in the possibilities of human nature, which was and is characteristic of many American communities, has been usually credited to our natural experience in the unlimited richness of an unexploited country. A realistic study of the frontier makes this explanation often doubtful, and sometimes ridiculous. The mild but pervasive influence of the Quakers is a more probable cause, although that influence was so widespread when America was in the making that by its very dilution it lost the name of Quaker. Certainly we felt it strongly in our school and our town, and to it must be charged some of our confidence in the world.

At first the academies, serving both boys and girls, were governed by the strictest rules. Boys and girls had only minimal opportunities to so much as speak to each other, and that under close faculty supervision. Today, in most of the boarding schools these rules have been considerably relaxed, though emphasis on curfew controls remain standard. A few of the schools have experimented with the honor system, but the majority remain conservative on this point.

One constant aspect of Quaker education has been the emphasis on providing schooling for persons of all races and religions. For many years the Quakers were the only group concerned with schools for the Negroes and the Indians. Although these schools were generally separate, Quakers sometimes admitted Negroes to their own schools when there were not enough Negro pupils to form a separate school.

In 1833 a young Quaker schoolmistress, Prudence Crandall, decided to admit a Negro girl to her girls' school in Canterbury, Connecticut. When the town fathers objected to this step, she resolved that rather than dismiss the Negro, Sarah Harris, she would dismiss all the white girls. Thereafter by means of advertisements in William Lloyd Garrison's *Liberator* and other abolitionist newspapers she gathered a student body of young Negro girls from many states to fill up her school. The incensed townspeople threw garbage on her stoop, fouled her well, drove her from the church, and broke all her windows. Finally they managed to persuade the Connecticut legislature to pass a law against a school "for the instruction and education of colored persons who are not inhabitants of this state." Prudence was found guilty, and though an appeal was sought for her, it became impossible for her to continue to conduct her school in the face of the inflexible hostility of the town.

This story has a happy ending. Many years later the state of Connecticut voted Prudence Crandall a life pension, expunged from the record her conviction as a criminal, and apologized for the "cruel outrages" inflicted upon a former citizen.

After World War II, Quaker schools and colleges were among the first private institutions to desegregate both student bodies and faculties, though not all of these institutions were equally diligent. Today most of them have programs for identifying talented boys and girls from among the underprivileged in their own communities and providing them with scholarships so that the student body may represent a diversity in social and economic class as well as in race.

Many Quakers of tender conscience worry today about the validity of their maintaining private schools at all, particularly in metropolitan areas where the public schools badly need the leaven of superior students and deeply concerned parents.

Quaker schools have a right to continue, many feel, only if they find more and more ways to share their assets with the whole community. To that end the Friends Council on Education, a group representing all the Quaker schools and colleges, is experimenting with ways to provide extra leadership, teachers, volunteers, and enrichment to slum schools in the Philadelphia area. In Detroit a group of Quakers is operating an interracial school in a slum area.

### QUAKER SCIENTISTS

The inductive approach of Quakers to religion flowered naturally into an interest in science which has long been associated with the Society. A number of Quakers have been eminent scientists as well as eminent physicians. In addition, hundreds of others have pursued science as a hobby. Many wealthy Quaker merchants of colonial Philadelphia dabbled in mathematics, astronomy, and botany. Among modern Quakers an interest in nature is characteristic.

There are interesting reasons for this preoccupation. For one thing, Quakers did not allow themselves any of the diversions of their day. Cock fighting, bull baiting, drinking bouts, stage-plays, cards, dice, May-games, masks, revels, and the like—all these amusements of the seventeenth and eighteenth centuries were frowned upon. Later this Puritan attitude hardened into a strong and unfortunate rejection of art, music, theater, and all works of fiction. There was really nothing left for the leisure hours but a study of natural phenomena. Secondly, Friends regarded the Truth as one and indivisible. Without being pantheistic, they felt that it was as important to know the truth about the wing of a bird as about any aspect of human society.

William Penn was himself elected to the Royal Society of London, less for any specific scientific research than for the generally scientific temper of his writing and his social experiment. His clerk, James Logan, who came to Philadelphia with him in 1699, became an eminent Quaker scientist as an avocation. He studied mathematics, astronomy, and optics and did painstaking research on the pollination of Indian corn.

A protégé of Logan, John Bartram, is regarded as America's first botanist. In 1728 he founded in Philadelphia the first botanical garden in America. His collection of native plants was probably the finest in the United States, and he was one of the first botanists to produce a hybrid. Bartram was one of five Quakers who were among the nine founding members of the American Philosophical Society, formed by the ubiquitous Benjamin Franklin in 1743. Unfortunately he was shortly thereafter accused of being a Deist, and disowned by his local meeting.

Another famous Quaker scientist of this period was Thomas Gilpin, the zoologist. John Bartram's son, William Bartram, is said to be the first American ornithologist. In the nineteenth century Edward Drinker Cope was a famous paleontologist who found the fossils of dinosaurs in the American West, while William James Beal is remembered for his contribution to the field of plant genetics. Maria Mitchell, a Nantucket Quaker, became America's first woman astronomer.

In Rhode Island the scientific temper among Quakers flowered in the activities of Moses Brown, a merchant who is remembered for his relief work during the Revolutionary War, his abolitionist activities, and his part in founding both Brown University and Moses Brown School. Brown experimented with astronomy and surveying as a hobby, dabbled in medicine, studied the possible cause of yellow fever, and worked to promote inoculation for smallpox. His greatest contribution, however, was the study of industrial methods which led him to bring the Arkwright water wheel to the new world, thus giving birth to the cotton industry in New England.

Many Quakers of a scientific bent have turned to medicine on both sides of the Atlantic. In England the most famous of these was Joseph Lister, founder of modern antiseptic surgery. In America Dr. Thomas Cadwallader was the first man to perform a scientific autopsy; Dr. Edward Jones wrote the first book on surgery, and perhaps the first book on any medical subject, to be published in America. Thomas and Phineas Bond helped to found the Pennsylvania Hospital.

Through the years American Quakers have continued to be prominent in both scientific inquiry and medicine. In 1968 the chairman of the board of the American Friends Service Committee was a world-renowned geographer, Dr. Gilbert F. White. The marriage between scientific ability and social concern is not accidental, but grows from deep Quaker roots. Many modern Quaker scientists are members of the Society for Social Responsibility in Science, a group which endeavors to promote ways to use such new scientific developments as nuclear power to human ends.

Someone has estimated that the Society of Friends has at least ten times as many scientists as one would expect to find in any group of similar numerical composition. This does not include the Quaker doctors, who are also numerous and who are to be found in the universities, working overseas and in this country in public health and all the branches of medicine. A circle of Quaker doctors has lately been meeting to consider new approaches to the population explosion and to the need for family planning.

Modern Quakers also pursue scientific interests as an avocation. They are great bird watchers, builders of nature trails, campers, and hikers. Around the turn of the century well-to-do Quakers began to go up into the Pocono Mountains of Pennsylvania in search of unspoiled country in which to teach their children the joy of nature. As a result, many of the hotels and resorts in that area were, and are, Quaker operated. There are also a number of Quaker-run hotels along the Jersey shore. Today, many people send their children to Quaker-run camps in the Poconos and in Vermont.

## QUAKERS AND THE ARTS

Because of their fear of airy notions, strict Quakers for many years confined their reading to the Bible and to heavy tomes of Quaker history, with an occasional treatise on botany or mathematics to vary the diet. Nevertheless, Quakers have been prolific writers throughout their history. Large libraries, containing volume upon volume of history, biography, autobiography, philosophy, Bible study, devotional writing, Quaker genealogy, and a certain amount of more recent poetry and fiction are collected at Haverford, Swarthmore, and Earlham colleges.

Many of the early Quakers kept journals recording their experiences with the Truth, detailing their travels, their travails, and sometimes their deepest feelings. Some of these journals are dull and pedestrian, but others are lit by vivid description and by wry flashes of humor. Many of them serve as valuable resources to historians, and a few are of use to the student of literature as well. The *Journal of John Woolman* is known for its purity of style and simplicity of expression, which transcend both provincialism and Quakerism to speak in a universal tongue. Penn's essays, *Some Fruits of Solitude,* were much admired by Robert Louis Stevenson and others for similar virtues.

The habit of writing exactly what one sees and feels is a valuable one for any writer. Walt Whitman, whose mother was a Quaker, put it into poetry in *Leaves of Grass:*

> You shall no longer take things at second or third hand, nor look through the eyes of the dead, nor feed on the spectres in books,

> You shall not look through my eyes either, nor take things
> from me,
> You shall listen to all sides and filter them from your self.

A Quaker heritage influenced other American writers in addition to Whitman. Both Thomas Paine and Benjamin Franklin had strong Quaker influence in their lives, the latter occasionally passing as a Quaker when it suited his purpose. James Fenimore Cooper grew up in a Quaker family. Both Emerson and Thoreau were influenced by Quaker ideas.

John Greenleaf Whittier was regarded as the brightest star in the Quaker literary world during the nineteenth century, though the judgment of time is that his was a minor, not a major, poetic gift. Another writer of the nineteenth century, Hannah Whitall Smith, wrote a book, *The Christian's Secret of a Happy Life*, which sold several million copies.

Quakers who have distinguished themselves in the twentieth century include Thomas R. Kelly, a mystic who wrote *Testament of Devotion*; Rufus Jones, a Quaker historian and a prolific writer on many subjects; and Dr. Elton Trueblood, also a writer on the subject of religion. Henry J. Cadbury, for many years teacher at the Harvard Divinity School, is regarded as one of the most distinguished Bible scholars of our day.

The twentieth century has also seen a blossoming in the field of fiction and of poetry, particularly by Quaker women. Elizabeth Gray Vining, the Quaker schoolteacher selected to tutor the Crown Prince of Japan, has written many books for children and adults, on Quaker and non-Quaker subjects. *Take Heed of Loving Me*, her book on John Donne, is perhaps her best-known work. Janet Whitney is known for her portraits of Quaker women. Jessamyn West's *The Friendly Persuasion* brought Quaker conflict in the Civil War to thousands of readers and hundreds of thousands of movie goers.

Though Quakers with literary talents found expression

through journal and history writing in the early days, incipient Quaker artists were wholly denied an outlet for more than one hundred years. Modern Friends regard their ancestors' disapproval of art and music as a tragic accident of history. The Puritans feared art as the work of the devil and believed that man could be corrupted by evil association with frivolous ideas. Since Quakerism grew out of Puritanism, it naturally tended to incorporate many Puritan concepts. Though the early Friends believed in the natural goodness of man they did not see the inconsistency of denying men and women natural forms of self-expression. Later when the Puritan movement itself was becoming less strict, the Quakers grew more rigid in their rejection of art as they withdrew from the world and became a peculiar people.

Nevertheless, the creative spirit occasionally broke through. Benjamin West is generally considered to have been born a Quaker, though there is some controversy on this point. Born in Springfield, Pennsylvania, in 1728, he taught himself to paint with homemade materials. In 1755 he set himself up as a portrait painter in Philadelphia, an unheard of thing for a Quaker to do in those days. Perhaps for this reason he rather quickly moved on to New York, and then to London, where he flourished and became famous.

It was in London that West painted his memorable picture of Penn's treaty with the Indians. Unfortunately he was by now so far from the scenes of his childhood that he forgot his Quaker history. Penn, who was a man in his vigorous forties at the time of the Treaty of Shackamaxon, is painted as old and stout.

A painter who was more typical of Quakerism of the Quietist era is Edward Hicks. Hicks was born in 1780, lost his mother a year later, and was raised by two Bucks County Quakers, Elizabeth and David Twining. At the age of thirteen he was apprenticed to a coach maker. Here Hicks learned lettering and decoration, a part of the coach making process, and discovered his love of painting.

In 1803 Hicks joined the Society of Friends, married, and shortly thereafter set up his own business as a painter of signs, coaches, and houses. He mixed his own paints, and during free moments in his workshop dabbled with landscapes. He was however, constantly torn about the propriety of Quaker painting. He wrote:

> If the Christian World was in the real spirit of Christ, I do not believe there would be such a thing as a fine painter in Christendom. It appears clearly to me to be one of those trifling, insignificant arts, which has never been any substantial advantage to mankind. But as the inseparable companion of voluptuousness and pride, it has presaged the downfall of empires and kingdoms; and in my view stands now enrolled among the premonitory symptoms of the rapid decline of the American Republic. But there is something of importance in the example of the primitive Christians and primitive Quakers to mind their callings of business, and work with their hands at such business as they are capable of, avoiding idleness and fanaticism.

Once he determined to give up painting forever and bought a farm intending to work it instead. But he was a failure as a farmer, and was forced back to his art in order to support himself and his family. Since he was a Quaker minister, taking long trips to the South, to Ohio, and to Canada, he had to work at high speed, turning out both pictures and signs on order. As a result his work never matured, and he is regarded today as one of the finest of the American primitives. His paintings of farm scenes, of Washington crossing the Delaware, of Biblical subjects, and of Penn's Treaty are all well known, but his finest work is "The Peaceable Kingdom," in which the lion lies down with the lamb.

One Quaker artist of the nineteenth century turned to sculpture. Eli Harvey, born in 1860 in Clinton County, Ohio, persisted in his efforts to learn to paint despite the disapproval of his Quaker community. He eventually earned enough money by painting local portraits to study in Paris, where he became interested in animal sculpture. He drifted away from the Society of Friends, but years later became interested in the little Friends meeting in Paris. His most famous piece, "Maternal Caress," portraying a lioness fondling her cub, was sculpted in this period. It is now in the Metropolitan Museum in New York.

The early Quakers objected to having their portraits painted. They preferred, they said, to be remembered for their deeds rather than their appearances. Gradually, however, they relaxed this testimony and permitted silhouettes, or shadow pictures, to be made of themselves and their loved ones. Today, what authentic pictures we have of prominent eighteenth- and nine-teenth-century Quakers are in profile. In addition many Quaker families have old silhouettes of their ancestors, snipped out by some clever aunt or cousin. The scissor art, as it was called, was regarded as a harmless pastime by the strict Quakers, and was consequently allowed as an innocent diversion for young Quaker boys and girls.

The effort of the Quakers to keep all their belongings simple and functional led them to achieve a certain aesthetic style as craftsmen, if not as fine artists. Early Quaker furniture makers, glass blowers, and silversmiths combined simplicity of line with careful work and produced household objects of a beautiful and simple style that fits in now with the best of twentieth-century interior design. The Quakers of the early eighteenth century built their meetinghouses as plainly as they knew how. The results are generally perfectly proportioned, pure uncluttered lines and the richness of old wood and stone against white walls.

The Quaker prohibition against music seems one of the saddest features of the history of the Society of Friends. It was for a time so complete that members were regularly disowned for dancing to a fiddle, for owning a musical instrument, or for joining in song. Yet the love of music of course could not be entirely removed from a people. The feelings of a young Quaker girl on this subject are aptly described in the diary of Rebecca Wright Hill:

> ... the last place we stopped at, on our journey, we met different fare. They were a family mostly grown, who were accustomed to and fond of society. We were welcomed as old friends. They all insisted that we should partake with them, and immediately set about preparing the evening repast, which consisted of two roast turkeys, venison, etc. of which we partook, both families sitting together. One of the sons entertained us with music from the violin. This was particularly relished by me as I was fond of music but this propensity had never been indulged. I was gratified that father sat and heard it without any visible signs of reluctance.

Today Quakers are as interested and involved in both music and fine arts as any other group. Quaker schools and colleges have fine arts and music departments, train choirs, and hold concerts and operatic performances. Since the 1880's the Quaker churches which hold a programed service have had singing and organ playing as a regular part of their worship. Most Quaker children learn to play a musical instrument, and there is music in the average Quaker home. There are now Quaker artists, architects, and city planners as well as Quaker poets and writers. A few of the former have made outstanding contributions to their field. Edmund Bacon is internationally known as a city planner, Sylvia Judson Haskins is regarded as a fine sculptress, and Fritz Eichenberg is famous for his woodcuts.

The Quaker prejudice against drama was even stronger than that against music. Invited to attend a lecture on Shakespeare, John Griscom, a Quaker teacher, said with some asperity:

> J. Griscom returns his sincere thanks for the kindness which prompted the invitation to attend a lecture at . . . Hall "upon Shakespeare." In the spirit of reciprocated comity he would beg leave to remark, that if the lecture is to be given for the purpose of demonstrating that the morals of mankind would be benefited by the entire extermination of the writings of the great British dramatist, he would be more inclined to attend it. That there may be many noble thoughts, many humane sentiments, many profound and correct exhibitions of human nature, which may be culled, as the bee gathers sweet from poisonous plants, from these writings, he would not deny. But that, taken in their totality, they demoralize society to a great extent is an opinion, whether right or wrong, he has long entertained.

In the twentieth century, however, even this prejudice has disappeared as completely as snow in summer. Today most Quakers keenly enjoy the theater, dramatics are taught in Quaker schools, and the talent of potential actors and playwrights is warmly encouraged. Dramatic skits and role playing are widely used in Quaker conferences, particularly as means for the understanding of other points of view, and subsequent reconciliation.

## QUAKERS AND GREAT IDEAS

If the Quakers contributed little to the history of fine arts in America, they have contributed much to the history of great ideas. Besides introducing such concepts as nonviolence and conscientious objection, they have helped to develop the national ideals of religious and civil liberty, of equality and of pure democracy. Several of these ideas deserve special treatment here.

The Quaker belief that there is "that of God in every man,"

and that every man's opinion is therefore important, has led them to take a long-standing interest in the maintenance of civil liberties. William Penn helped to establish the right of a jury to be free of judicial influence. Later, sections of his Frame of Government were used in writing the Bill of Rights. The principle of conscientious objection, first written into law in Rhode Island in colonial times, has been an important contribution to the concept of religious liberty.

The early Quakers objected to all oath taking, and won for themselves and any other group with similar scruples the right to affirm, rather than to swear. In addition they have been opposed to all loyalty oaths, not only because such oaths imply a double standard of morality, but because they invade the religious right of a man to think what he wishes in the privacy of his heart as long as he does not act in a manner detrimental to society. Furthermore, Quakers have questioned the practicality of such oaths in achieving their intention. As William Penn said: "The man who fears to tell untruth has no need to swear because he will not lie, while he that does not fear untruth, what is his oath worth?"

The seventeen Philadelphia Friends who refused to sign a loyalty oath during the Revolutionary War and were banished to Virginia as a result, based their refusal on the violation of civil liberties involved rather than any lack of enthusiasm for the Revolutionary cause. Later, when overzealous citizens of the new United States passed a law requiring a loyalty oath of all teachers, many Quakers resigned rather than affirm such an oath.

This testimony against loyalty oaths has been upheld consistently into the twentieth century. It has been Quakers, and not Communists, who have balked at taking the state loyalty oaths that popped out like measles during the McCarthy period, and Quaker suits have caused such oaths to be struck down by the federal courts. In April, 1966, when the Arizona law demanding a loyalty oath was found unconstitutional by the United States Supreme Court, the case tried was that of two Quaker junior high school teachers who had continued to teach without pay for five years while their case was being heard. Similar challenges have been made elsewhere, or are now under litigation.

In addition to challenging such laws themselves, the Quakers have defended the rights of others to take this position. The American Friends Service Committee administers a Rights of Conscience fund which supports people suffering job loss or other reprisals for taking unpopular views. Developed during the McCarthy era, this fund has also been used to help men and women in the South who have suffered because of their work in civil rights.

The American Civil Liberties Union, created directly after World War I, has always had the wholehearted support of Quakers, and several Quakers have been both board and staff members. This organization works to see that everyone enjoys the privileges of the Bill of Rights. It is therefore eager to guard the freedom of speech of an avowed American Fascist like the late George Lincoln Rockwell or a Communist such as Gus Hall. It also rigorously upholds the separation of church and state.

Deeply intertwined with the Quakers' concern for civil liberties has been their long struggle for religious liberty for themselves and others. Penn used the founding of his Holy Experiment as an opportunity to invite such persecuted minorities as the Mennonites to share the freedom of Pennsylvania. In the latter part of the nineteenth century, American and English Quakers cooperated with Count Leo Tolstoy in arranging for the Doukhobors, a primitive Christian group in Russia, to find sanctuary in Canada. At the end of World War II American

Quakers aided a Buddhist community, the Kalmuks, a persecuted minority for some nine hundred years, to settle in the United States.

Shortly after Pearl Harbor Day the decision was made by the United States Government to evacuate all persons of Japanese ancestry from the West Coast and remove them to relocation centers where they could remain while their loyalty was being cleared and while plans were made for their resettlement. The move was made precipitately, giving the men and women involved no time to close up their homes or their businesses.

The Quakers were among several religious groups deeply disturbed by this treatment of a large group of Americans—70 per cent of them citizens—whose loyalty was implicitly questioned on the basis of race. In the end only a handful were found to have enemy sympathies, but by this time over one hundred and ten thousand persons had been removed from their homes, businesses, and communities. Through the AFSC, the Quakers helped the Japanese Americans: in tying up loose threads at their hastily left homes, in relocating to new jobs, and in finding scholarships for their college-age young people. Throughout this period they continued to protest this infringement on the Bill of Rights.

Civil and religious liberties are not only rights unto themselves; they are widely regarded as essential to the functioning of a democracy based on the contribution of everyone's point of view. Is such a participatory democracy an ideal which can never be perfectly realized? Some scholars point to the Quaker business meeting as an example of the translation of this ideal into reality. Today modifications of the Quaker methods are being attempted in industry and government. The popular concept of consensus is related to the Quaker belief in the importance of obtaining a sense of the meeting before any action is taken. There are, however, important differences.

Since the Quakers make no distinction between their spiritual and their everyday life, they conduct their meetings for business in very much the same spirit as their meetings for worship. Business meetings begin with a period of silence, often deep and meaningful rather than perfunctory. Sometimes the meeting lapses into silence again in the course of discussion. This is apt to happen when the give and take becomes too heated, when a seeming impasse has been reached, or when one member speaks so eloquently that the group is moved.

Leading the discussion in a Quaker business meeting is the clerk, whose role it is to be sensitive to the wishes of the group. He tries to see to it that on important matters everyone present expresses himself. He must prevent a dominant member from exerting undue influence on the meeting, see that proper weight is given to the opinion of a member whose views are particularly pertinent to the subject at issue, and encourage the timid to speak up. He avoids expressing his own views. After what he believes to have been an adequate discussion he will try to phrase the sense of the meeting. "What I seem to be hearing is that we are agreed on appropriating the money for the new sidewalk," he may say, leaving room for those who object to say so. If there is no dissent, group approval is expressed, various members saying, "I agree with that" or "that speaks my mind." Like their forefathers, modern Quakers do not vote.

In a real sense the whole of Quaker childhood training and education prepares the individual for participation in this sort of democratic exercise. From childhood on Quakers are taught to say bluntly what is on their minds, rather than to hide latent conflict behind polite words. On the other hand they are also taught to subdue individual aggressiveness in the interest of the group, and to be as objective as possible in group discussion.

Even when deep issues are involved and thorny conflicts are being faced, the discussion at a Quaker business meeting sounds bland and low keyed to an outsider. There is a surprising amount of laughter, perhaps used for the release of tensions.

When an individual Quaker in a group meeting finds that the group seems to be deciding an issue in a manner with which he disagrees, he must search his conscience. Is his stand based on an objective view of the facts, informed by his individual conscience? Or is pride, insensitivity, or personal ambition in some way standing between himself and his ability to see the group's point of view? Only when he feels clear that his objection is based on valid grounds of conscience does he oppose himself to the group.

If one or more members decide in this fashion that they cannot agree, the decision is held over sometimes for months, sometimes for years, until time softens hard feelings, or until a new synthesis is possible on the basis of a new idea. Occasionally a subcommittee is asked to wrestle with a thorny issue in the hope that it can produce the new spurt needed to solve the problem. The subcommittee must, however, report back to the full group, and cannot therefore be used as a dodge.

The process of reaching a decision in this fashion is slow, and does not always work. In order to reach apparent unity, meetings sometimes do not bring their conflicts sufficiently out into the open, and wallpaper over their differences. Nevertheless, Friends continue to feel that when a true sense of the meeting is achieved, the results are well worth the extra effort and time involved.

Once a Quaker meeting makes a decision in proper fashion, that decision has the wholehearted support of all its members. There is no bitter minority to nurse its defeat and to sabotage the new project. The decision finally taken is generally not a compromise, but a new idea, both more encompassing and more creative than those previously advanced. The wrestling that goes on while a meeting waits for such an idea may have something to do with the Quaker reputation for coming up with unexpected and practical solutions to thorny problems.

In the spring of 1967 the small meetinghouse of Conscience Bay Meeting at St. James, New York, ' heard a fellow Quaker from Philadelphia call for an end to the Vietnam war. During the following week vandals smeared ugly accusations of disloyalty on its white walls: "Treason! Traitors! There can be no compromise with Commies! $10,000 for V.C. a Knife in the Back for American G.I.'s. The American Dead will be avenged! This is a God-is-Dead so-called Church." Everywhere the walls were disfigured with a rash of stenciled red hammer-and-sickle designs.

During a long business meeting, full of turbulent feelings, the members of the meeting decided what their response to this action should be. Should they give the act wide publicity? Or should they say nothing, and meekly repair the damage? Or call the police? Or leave the signs for all to see? The meeting was deeply divided between those who wanted to use the occasion to protest the illiberalism of the vandals and those who wanted no publicity. One man in particular felt strongly that nothing should be released to the papers. Feeling ran high, and several times the clerk had to ask the meeting to settle into silence. Finally, after a particularly long and deep period of silence, the man who had opposed publicity came up with a new idea. Why not invite the friends and neighbors of Conscience Bay Meeting to join with its members in repairing the damage? The invitation could be issued through the medium of the press, but it would create positive, not negative, publicity.

The idea, endorsed enthusiastically by the meeting and published in *The New York Times* and other papers, caught on quickly. Groups from neighboring churches and civic groups volunteered to help. Persons called the Quakers to say, "I'm opposed to your stand on the war in Vietnam but I want to help paint the meetinghouse." A successful paint-in with more than two hundred persons present was held the next Sunday.

This is just one small example of something that has happened over and over again in Quaker history; the emergence from group struggle of a new and better idea. The "sweet unity" which Friends cherish is gained not by compromise but by creativity. Quakers occasionally but only rarely confuse the two.

Will the Quaker method work for other groups? Ideally a Quaker meeting is made up of individuals who have been taught from childhood to express their feelings openly and to avoid dominant, aggressive behavior. These individuals have known each other often over long periods of time, hold similar values, and are bound together by ties of affection and commonly held ideals. All these qualities are hard to duplicate in other situations. Moreover, the Quakers themselves point out that their method is based on a commonly shared belief in a unifying Presence which each meets in the silence of the period of worship.

Nevertheless, modifications of the Quaker method have been put to work in business, in the United Nations, in international conferences. The Quakers themselves have had considerable success in using the techniques of the Quaker business meeting in their efforts to reconcile opposed groups—in labor relations, in race relations, and in the field of international diplomacy. The attitude of openness toward other points of view, the patient search for unity beneath diversity, the avoidance of polarization —and the agendas, written statements, and votes that lead to polarization of opposing views—have helped the Quakers gain their reputation as the world's peacemakers.

## ❧ 9
# Quakers and
# the world

The Quaker movement began with an explosion of missionary activity. The early Friends felt called upon to carry their message to the far corners of the earth. For the first quarter century, individual Quakers traveled far and wide, visiting Germany, Holland, and ports along the Mediterranean. One Quaker called on the Sultan, and another, the Pope in Rome. Settlements of Quakers in Barbados and in the new colonies were a result of this early zeal.

Years of persecution served to quench these first fires and to turn the Quakers inward. Public Friends continued to speak to gatherings until the middle of the eighteenth century, but there was progressively less of this activity as Quietism began to settle upon the Society. Visits to the Indians, at first a matter of individual concern, became a group responsibility in the nineteenth century.

A faith is hard to maintain unless it is shared. The decline of Quakerism in the first part of the nineteenth century was probably connected with this atrophy of outreach. When the evangelical movement swept the American frontier after the Civil War, one of its great appeals to the Quakers was a rebirth of the missionary spirit. In consequence, at the same time many meetings turned to programed services, they also began to establish missionary outposts with a strong evangelical flavor.

The first Quaker group in the United States to support a foreign mission was the New England Yearly Meeting. In 1869 Eli and Sybil Jones, on a trip to Palestine, met a young woman who said she wanted to teach in a girls' school. Satisfied that she was indeed a qualified teacher, the Joneses agreed to advance her a sum of money. The Quaker school in Ramallah, so founded, has continued to this day.

Other groups followed New England's lead. In 1871, Indiana sent a man to Mexico, and in 1881, Iowa dispatched missionary workers to Jamaica. Ohio developed missions in China and India; New York became interested in Mexico; Kansas took on Alaska. Though Philadelphia Yearly Meeting, maintaining its policy of isolation, did not become involved in missionary activity as such, a group of women became interested in starting a girls' school in Japan.

In 1894, a number of yearly meetings joined to form the American Friends Board of Missions. This group in turn sponsored mission work in Cuba, where it was discovered that two independent religious groups had spontaneously developed along

Quaker lines after some Cubans read Quaker literature translated into Spanish by the missionaries in Mexico. The Friends developed five schools in Cuba, and operated them until they were nationalized by Castro in 1961.

In 1902, three young Friends, graduates of the Cleveland Bible Institute, became interested in starting a mission among the Abaluhya tribe in British East Africa. This effort was so startlingly successful that today there are some 32,000 Quakers in East Africa, chiefly in Kenya, with seventy-six monthly and fourteen quarterly meetings. East Africa Yearly Meeting is the largest in the world.

During the nineteenth century, before this missionary effort took shape, American Quakers were beginning to concern themselves more actively with the problems of creating world peace. They had always been pacifists, but now they began to see that something more was required of them than abstaining from involvement in violence. They must in fact help to create a warless world.

Following the War of 1812, Quakers both in England and the United States began to help in the formation of local and national peace societies. The purpose of these groups was at first somewhat diffuse and vague, but became more crystallized as large international peace congresses were held by the constituent societies: Boston in 1841, London in 1843, Brussels in 1848, Paris in 1849, and Frankfurt in 1850. These gatherings advocated with increasing firmness a Congress of Nations and a Court of Nations to settle international disputes. The vision of William Penn one hundred and fifty years before was revived. Quakers attending these congresses spoke up for the idea of sending small international delegations to various capitals to help negotiate various delicate situations, but the general membership of these gatherings was not ready to take such "political" action.

In the United States another interesting development was taking place. This was the wedding between the abolitionist movement and the philosophy of nonviolence. In 1838, William Lloyd Garrison broke off from the American Peace Society to found the New England Non-Resistance Society. Lucretia Mott was a member, but since it was regarded as a "mixed association," it was eschewed by many Friends. Garrison and his followers, nevertheless, leaned heavily on accounts of early Quaker experiences with the Indians to bolster their position.

Influenced in turn by Garrison and others, Henry David Thoreau took the developing idea of nonviolence one step further when he refused to pay the Massachusetts poll tax in 1846 as a protest against the war in Mexico. His essay on "Civil Disobedience," written after he spent a night in jail, eventually influenced Tolstoy, Gandhi, and the late Reverend Martin Luther King, Jr.

American Quakers were united with Thoreau in opposing the war with Mexico, on both religious and moral grounds. They sent Congress a memorial outlining the Quaker objection to all war, and their particular unhappiness about this one. Like many of their fellow Americans, they saw it as an effort to extend slavery and to impose the American will on a helpless people. In 1898, they made a similar strong objection to the Spanish-American War.

The Civil War swept most of the early peace societies out of existence. At the same time almost all of the abolitionists promptly renounced their allegiance to nonviolence. The American Quakers found themselves alone to wrestle with their consciences in regard to participation in the war, to try to obtain the rights of conscience for their sons who refused to fight, and to find ways to aid the war sufferers. After the war, the job of educating and caring for the freed slaves absorbed their energies for several decades.

Meanwhile, English Friends were becoming engaged in the work for which all Quakers are now best known—the tasks of war relief. After the Crimean War, Friends and others in England were shocked to learn that the British fleet had laid waste the towns and villages of Finland along the shores of the Gulf of Bothnia and the Baltic Sea. Raising a sum of £9,000, the Quakers sent a small team to distribute clothes, food, provisions for shelter, fishing nets, and seed corn.

A much larger project of war service was undertaken by the British Friends during and after the Franco-Prussian War in 1870. Hearing about the suffering of noncombatants, particularly in Alsace and Lorraine, the English Quakers sent some twenty-five unarmed workers into the war zones to see what could be done. Later these volunteers helped civilians during the siege of Paris and extended their operations as far as the Loire valley. It was during this period that the red-and-black star, now a famous Quaker symbol around the world, was first used by the Friends.

English Quakers, opposed to the Boer War on several counts, were horrified to learn of the treatment of the Afrikaans women and children in the concentration camps. The reports of Emily Hobhouse, an English nurse in South Africa, prompted the Quakers to send a small team to investigate. Their findings led them to obtain from the British Government permission to distribute food and medical supplies to the women and children in the camps. Maintaining their traditional neutrality, they also provided services for some English refugee families in the Transvaal. The South Africans remember this wartime service to this day, and tolerate the small Quaker minority who live in their country and continue to seek ways to oppose the racial injustice of apartheid.

All these experiences in war service were the forerunners of the development of two great sister organizations: the American Friends Service Committee and the Friends Service Council of London. Developed during World War I to meet the needs of the time, the two have continued ever since to perform acts of humanitarian service around the world. In 1947 they received jointly the Nobel Peace Prize. The AFSC is the only American organization ever to be so honored.

The creation of the two service bodies in wartime was motivated by two concerns: the desire of Quakers to give war relief and their need for finding alternative service for conscientious objectors. In both England and America the compulsory draft laws were harsh toward CO's. In England the local tribunals were not disposed to grant CO's alternative service, and some six thousand young men were in consequence imprisoned. In the United States all the CO's (except for the absolutists) were drafted into the army, then furloughed to alternative service such as farm labor. This did not always work out in practice, however. The young American conscientious objectors often found that their commanding officers did not understand the provisions for their exemption from military duties. In some cases their refusal to bear arms was regarded as a discipline problem, and they were placed in army prisons and—in a few cases—beaten for insubordination. Five hundred were court martialed and convicted, seventeen were sentenced to death (but not actually executed), and 142 were given life imprisonment, later commuted.

In the face of the public hostility that lay behind this harshness, young Quakers began to look for alternative service that would make it clear to their fellow countrymen that they were not cowards, but operated on a different principle. On April 30, 1917, representatives from all major Quaker groups met at the Young Friends Association in Philadelphia to see if they could establish "a service of love in wartime." A committee was organized, officers were selected, and various service projects considered.

"We are united in expressing our love of our country and our desire to serve her loyally," the group said in a recorded minute. "We offer our services to the Government of the United States in any constructive work in which we can conscientiously serve humanity."

The American Friends Service Committee, so organized, has been from the beginning the creation of many men and women working together. In its inception and early days, however, it gained strength from one guiding spirit. This was Rufus M. Jones, a Quaker from South China, Maine, a professor at Haverford College, and perhaps the most remarkable man the Society of Friends produced in the twentieth century. Warm, witty, full of anecdotes, he was a prolific speaker and writer. He edited the magazine, *The American Friend,* wrote volumes of Quaker history, and helped to draw New England, southern, and midwestern Friends into a new alliance—the Five Years Meeting— in 1902. He saw the creation of the AFSC as an opportunity to unite all the branches of American Friends in a common service project. It was Rufus Jones who chaired the early meetings and who subsequently served as either chairman or honorary chairman of the board from 1917 to 1948.

The constructive work finally agreed upon by the government, the AFSC, and the Red Cross, was the formation of a Reconstruction Unit for service abroad. Trained at Haverford College, the young conscientious objectors—some Quakers, Mennonites, Brethren, and others—went to France to join the British Friends. Others, who were for one reason or another exempt from the draft, went, too, and a number of young women joined the Unit. At its high-water mark, there were some 600 workers in

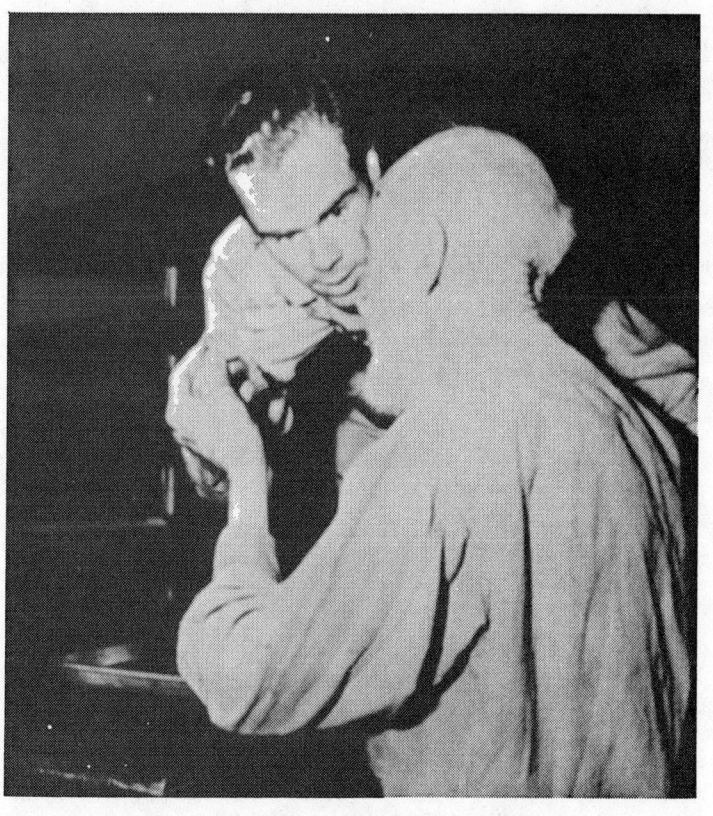

A conscientious objector feeds a ninety-five-year-old man in a mental hospital. (*Photo by De Vigne.*)

AFSC workers in Buzuluk, Province of Samara, Russia, in 1921, during the great Russian famine. (*Courtesy the American Friends Service Committee.*)

France, wearing the gray uniform of the Red Cross with the red-and-black star of Quaker service on their sleeves.

In France, the reconstruction workers were divided into teams, and assigned to a variety of wartime services. Some helped the British Friends operate the various hospitals and children's homes that had been placed under Quaker care, some built portable wooden houses for the refugees, some aided the French farmers in reclaiming war-abandoned fields. Others distributed food, clothing, and bedding to the homeless, and helped establish sewing and embroidery workshops for idle refugee women.

Six American workers managed to get to Russia by way of Japan and Siberia. In the Buzuluk region north of the Caspian Sea they joined a team of twenty-six British workers already at work in war relief. In 1890 and again in 1907, the English Quakers had helped in this area in time of famine. Now they were back, trying to deal with the human flood of refugees pouring in from the West. Together, American and English workers provided emergency food, clothing, and medical care, tried to unite families separated in the long trek, established self-help projects in refugee camps, and cared for orphaned and abandoned children. They worked until October, 1918, when they were advised to leave because of the Revolution. In Omsk, Siberia, they spent the winter, trying to help the people who now fled before the revolutionary forces. The Quakers lived in a fourth class railroad coach on a siding in a freight yard, and visited the shelters which the refugees had dug for themselves in the snow. In May of 1919 they left via Vladivostok, and after many adventures, arrived safely home.

In Europe, meanwhile, the end of the war brought the Quaker teams an opportunity to try out the ideas for reconstruction which they had developed in training back at Haverford. In France, they were given the entire Verdun area, comprising some forty villages, in which to supervise the rebuilding of farms, houses, and schools. They found an opportunity to turn swords into plowshares quite literally by buying up five large dumps of leftover army surplus and salvaging the materials for reconstruction purposes. They sold a carload of bayonets to a farm-tool manufacturer to be melted down for metal plows.

Working in close connection with both the American and French armies, the Quakers found they had many moral dilemmas to resolve in this period. One of the stickiest was the question of using German war prisoners in the reconstruction work. The French had these men at work on road building and other projects without pay, and offered the Friends as many of these workers as they could use. The Quakers debated, then decided to accept the offer as long as they did not accept the free labor. Instead, they kept account of every hour the Germans worked for them. Later, other Quaker workers went to Germany and paid the families the withheld wages. This money, coming at a time when Germany was suffering from poverty and inflation, seemed to some of the families like a gift from heaven.

In the months directly after the Armistice, rumors of conditions within Germany drifted out to disturb many sensitive people, the Quakers among them. The shortages produced by the war, magnified by the Allied Blockade, were producing widespread malnutrition among the German children. In 1919, three AFSC representatives visited Germany on the first civilian passports to be issued since the signing of the peace. Their findings confirmed the worst rumors—a whole generation showed the effects of hunger in rickets, ill health, and despair. The American Quakers were considering how to respond to this situation when an unexpected communication came from Herbert Hoover, chairman of the American Relief Administration. Would they take charge of the distribution of food to children in Germany?

Feeding German children, 1920
(*Courtesy the American Friends Service Committee.*)

AFSC worker confers with Indians in the sagebrush country. (*Photo by Ted Hetzel.*)

This was relief on a far larger scale than the Quakers had ever attempted, but with a burst of practical energy they rose to the occasion. By January a team was in Germany. By February, feeding had begun. By June of 1921 the AFSC was at work in 1,640 communities feeding 1,100,658 children and pregnant and nursing mothers. Meals were supplied by central kitchens. Each person certified by a doctor as needing extra food received 750 calories a day. This, on top of the official government ration of 1,300 calories, made the difference between health and illness for thousands and thousands of children. Many German towns, printing new currency to meet the demands of inflation, stamped their coins "Quaker Dank" in gratitude for the feeding.

In Austria and Poland the Quaker Service workers also went, helping to supply milk for tubercular children, to fight typhus, to reclaim the land. In Serbia they built houses, in Syria they maintained schools and provided medical care, in Bulgaria they distributed seeds and tools, and in Albania and Poland they established agricultural schools. As the reconstruction work progressed, it became clear that the Quakers had a special flair for this sort of practical humanitarian work.

In 1921, word reached the outside world that famine conditions threatened the Volga region in Russia. Some of the Quaker workers already busy on projects elsewhere in Europe were recruited and sent to the area, where they found the situation even worse than it had been reported. As winter deepened, the peasants ate the thatch of their cottages, their farm animals, the birds, and the mice. Hundreds died of starvation and of typhus which raged through the famine-weakened population. Two members of the Quaker unit became ill and were nursed back to health by their exhausted companions. The AFSC volunteers reported that the hardest thing of all was to force themselves to eat while men and women literally starved on their doorstep. It was, however, necessary for them to keep going in order to distribute the carloads of grain sent by generous American groups.

One peril was the bandits, who roamed the Russian plains in these unsettled times. Another was the Soviet soldiers, also wandering rather freely in this period, who offered to protect the Quakers from the bandits. Both groups wanted to be fed, but the Quakers refused, insisting that the food must go only to children and nursing mothers. In most cases this refusal was honored and the Quakers went about their work with food committees as first bandits, and then soldiers, and then bandits again took control of the town.

Though they did not know it at the time, the Quakers in all these projects were establishing a pattern of relief work that was to become characteristic of their operations. First, a short period of direct relief—feeding, clothing, and medical care—until emergency needs were met. Then, as soon as feasible, a self-help program in which the dignity and initiative of uprooted persons was supported and their self-respect regained. Then the establishment of some sort of training institution so that local people might be ready to take over the Quaker initiated projects. As soon as this third step was taken, the Quakers removed themselves from the situation as quickly as possible. They wanted, above all things, to avoid creating dependency.

As a result of this pattern, the Quaker workers found themselves, in the mid-twenties, in various stages of devolving the operations of a maternity hospital in France, a home for tubercular children in Austria, and an agricultural school in Poland. Though they withdrew as quickly as they could from these projects, some oversight was needed from time to time. Also, though it had never been the AFSC intention, converts had been made in several of the major cities of Europe. Watching the Quaker workers in action, some war-weary men and women had found something to believe in again.

As a result of all these threads holding it to Europe, the AFSC established small international centers in Paris, Berlin, Vienna, Geneva, Warsaw, and Moscow. A director, often a man and his wife, was appointed by either the British or American Friends to serve as a host to the center. Naturally enough, these centers became places where people interested in better international relations and in world peace could meet and encourage one another.

Through their international centers, the American Quakers kept in sensitive touch with the troubles in Europe at a time when the majority of their fellow citizens were turning to isolationism. By the early 1930's these centers were registering signs of the coming storm. In 1934 the Quaker staff at the Vienna center fed the families of some eight thousand workers, largely Social Democrats, who lost their jobs in the uprising in February, and then later also fed the families of the Nazis who were thrown in jail by Dolfuss after the July Putsch. In the same year the Berlin center became a focal point for Jews who wanted to emigrate to the United States, while the Paris center coped with the problems of some four thousand refugee families.

When the Spanish Civil War broke out, the AFSC helped in both the Loyalist and the Nationalist territories, feeding children and providing emergency services for the refugees. After the Loyalist opposition collapsed, the Quakers went with the refugees over the snow-topped Pyrenees into France. Here the Service Committee kept workers for many years, helping the refugees who lived in hastily constructed camps around Montauban.

Even while the AFSC was deeply involved in trying to help the victims of the Spanish Civil War, the mounting persecution of the Jewish people in Hitler's Germany began to absorb the time and energy of the international staff.

Following the Day of Broken Glass, November 10, 1938, an American Jewish group approached the Quakers to see if they might consider undertaking a feeding program for German Jews, whose shops were wrecked and who were forbidden to shop in Gentile stores.

Shortly thereafter, three Quakers set off for Berlin to investigate the situation. When they arrived, Jewish leaders there pleaded with them to forget about food and concentrate on arranging for emigration. Finding that they could do nothing without the permission of the Gestapo, the three arranged for an audience with a top official of that notorious group. They thus became the only American church group to make a direct appeal to the Nazis to cease their persecution of the Jews.

The Quakers had asked to see Himmler, but they were received by subordinates of Heydrich "the Hangman." According to their accounts, the two stony-faced SS men met them and read impassively the document they had prepared. In this statement the Quakers told of their work in feeding German children after World War I and stated that they came now in the same spirit. After a prolonged discussion of the program which the Quakers proposed now to undertake, the two SS men withdrew to consult with chief Heydrich. Left alone in the conference room at this solemn juncture, the three Quakers settled spontaneously into a deep silence.

The two men returned after almost half an hour and announced that everything the Quakers had asked had been granted. Could they have that in writing, the leader of the group asked? No, the Nazis said, that wouldn't be necessary. Every word spoken in the room was recorded. The Quakers looked at each other, very glad they had kept their Quaker silence.

It is hard to gauge the results of this visit. For some months after it took place, Quakers working in Germany felt they were given additional freedom in making emigration arrangements for Jewish families and in bringing relief. It was, however, only a drop of comfort in an ocean of need.

For the next few years the Quakers threw all their resources into work for the refugees. A small staff labored fiercely in Berlin, trying to cope with the constant lines of desperate people outside the Quaker center. Offices were opened in Rome, Lisbon, Amsterdam, Vienna, and Madrid, later in Copenhagen and Japan. Within the United States the Quakers operated hostels and language camps for the new refugees, and Quaker meetings all across the country sponsored new families needing assimilation. In all, some fifty thousand refugees were helped by the Quakers. They were mainly people who were not eligible for help from other agencies—partners in mixed marriages or persons with no religious affiliation.

Until the curtain of war fell completely on Europe, the AFSC stayed on, still trying to get a few last families out of Germany, to feed the children of France during the Allied Blockade, to continue to care for the Spanish refugees in southern France. When the United States entry into the war finally forced the Quaker workers out, they set up headquarters among the European refugees in Morocco, Algeria, and Santo Domingo. Some volunteers did not leave in time, and were interned during the war. European Quakers kept the little Quaker centers going during the darkest hours.

Throughout the war years, the drafted conscientious objectors were not permitted out of the country. A few, exempt from the draft for one reason or another, went to China where they served in the Friends Ambulance Unit, convoying medical supplies and later offering war relief on both sides of the Chinese Civil War.

Others served in India, where the AFSC was asked to help during the famine of 1944. The majority, however, spent their years in remote civilian public service camps, or in mental hospitals, and awaited the end of hostilities before going overseas.

Quaker workers were as active in reconstruction work after World War II as they had been after World War I. In the intervening twenty-five years, however, many other church, welfare, and labor groups had become engaged in relief work, and the Friends were no longer alone in the field. In consequence the AFSC no longer tried to meet all the needs of the dislocated but developed specialized services—small community centers in Germany, France, and Japan; small industries in Finland; transport in Italy. It was on the basis of this work, as well as its long history in relief, that the AFSC (along with the British FSC) received the Nobel Peace Prize in 1947.

In making the award, Gunnar Jahn, chairman of the Nobel Committee, gave a twentieth-century interpretation of the Quaker peace testimony:

> The fact that Quakers have refused to take part in war has led many people to believe that this is the essential part of their religion. But the matter is not quite so simple. It is true that the declaration of 1660 contains the following words: "We utterly deny all outward wars and strife and fighting with outward weapons to any end and under any pretense whatever. This is our testimony to the whole world." In this declaration there is implied much more than a mere refusal to take part in war. It amounts to the following: It is better to suffer injustice than to exercise injustice. In the end victory must come from within the individual man or woman. . . .
>
> It is the silent help from the nameless to the nameless which is their contribution to the promotion of brotherhood among nations. . . . This is the message of good deeds, the

message that men can come into contact with one another in spite of war and in spite of difference of race. May we believe that here there is hope of laying a foundation for peace among nations, of building up peace in man himself, so that it becomes impossible to settle disputes by use of force?

There was no time, however, for the Quakers to rest on these laurels. In 1947 the establishment of independence for India was followed by the tragedy of communal rioting and trouble in the Punjab and Kashmir. AFSC workers negotiated between the two groups and rescued stranded pockets of Moslems or Hindus surrounded by hostile majorities. Indians of both persuasions seemed to feel that the presence of one unarmed Quaker worker was as good a protection as a small detachment of troops in passing through hostile territory.

The next year the Quakers were invited to help maintain peace in Jerusalem as independence for Israel and the withdrawal of the British approached. The Arabs and the Jews agreed at one point that the only person who would be acceptable to both groups as municipal commissioner (or mayor) was Clarence Pickett, then the executive secretary of the AFSC. Since Pickett was not free to leave, another Quaker, Harold Evans, was appointed in his place. Before his ship reached Palestine, however, warfare broke out. For eighteen months the AFSC took charge of feeding some 200,000 Arab refugees in the Gaza strip in cooperation with the United Nations. At the same time, to maintain their policy of neutrality, the Quakers fed refugees in Galilee. Later, the Service Committee helped both Jordan and Israel improve their agriculture. In 1967, after the Arab-Israeli war, the AFSC was invited back by both sides.

During the fifties and the sixties the AFSC was kept busy, responding to the world's continuing crises. In 1953, the Committee sent medical teams to Korea. In 1956, it was asked to help when the Hungarian Revolution caused refugees to pour into Austria and Yugoslavia. In 1959, the Quakers sent a small staff to Hong Kong to aid the Chinese refugees. At the same time, teams went to Morocco and Tunisia to aid the Algerian refugees. In October, 1966, the AFSC opened a day care center, and a year later a rehabilitation center in South Vietnam, and sent a small amount of medical supplies to North Vietnam. Throughout this period the AFSC continued to find new homes for refugees—from the displaced persons camps of Europe, from Indo-China, from Cuba—and to work for a better immigration policy.

Because of a backlog of goodwill created by these activities, the AFSC has been able in the past fifteen years to gather diplomats from all over the world into informal, off-the-record conferences. Started in Europe in 1952, these conferences are now held annually in Africa, Europe, and Asia, as well as the United States. Diplomats from many nations are invited to each conference, and it has not been unusual for the Quakers to persuade Israeli and Arab, Indian and Pakistani, to meet under these circumstances. Wives and children are encouraged to attend, and there is plenty of time for recreation. Since no formal resolutions are adopted and no votes taken, the effort is made in the discussion of international issues to seek points of agreement, rather than disagreement.

The result of all this is that many of the diplomats relax, and come to know each other as persons, rather than as stereotypes.

How much carry-over there is from these conferences to the actual diplomatic conference table is difficult to judge. The conferences themselves grow in popularity each year, and the alumni get together for frequent reunions. More than one hundred and fifty of the diplomats who have attended the conferences are now of ambassadorial rank. Altogether one-tenth of the world's diplomats have taken part in the Quaker gatherings.

In addition to the diplomats' conferences, the AFSC arranges international seminars for graduate students, affiliations and exchanges between schools in the United States and seven nations abroad, international work camps, and off-the-record conversations in Washington, New York, and Geneva. At a time of special international tension, it sends missions to the world's capitals to talk to the diplomats known to the Quakers and to urge peace.

Just as Quaker concern sent Mary Fisher to see the Sultan in 1660 and Eliza Gurney to visit Abraham Lincoln in 1862, it prompted both English and American Friends to call upon the rulers of Russia several times during the nineteenth century. Picking up on this long tradition the AFSC sent the mission to Germany in 1938, a mission to Moscow in the early days of the Cold War, a mission to divided Berlin in 1963, and one to India and Pakistan in 1966.

Ground for the mission to Berlin was prepared by a Quaker sociologist Roland Warren, who spent several years passing back and forth through the Berlin Wall, looking for areas of agreement and ways to keep communication open. Almost everyone with whom Roland Warren talked remembered something about the Quaker feeding of German children after World War I, and this gave him an opportunity to talk to many people who might not otherwise have spared the time. He was able to discuss with both East and West German officials their positions on reunification, being careful never to say one thing to one group and another to the other, or to sound as though he were taking sides. The two antagonists, he discovered, had a mirror image of the other. That is, each saw the other as intransigent, aggressive, and unreasonable. By presenting one side to the other he was occasionally able to shake up some of the stereotyped thinking, and to start conversations. His work, and that of his successor, is typical of the sort of one-man private, quiet diplomacy the Quakers attempt in the trouble spots of the world.

One of the conditions leading to war in the modern world is the disparity between the wealth of the developed nations and the poverty of the underdeveloped lands. During the past twenty-five years, the AFSC has had projects of community development in India, Pakistan, Mexico, Peru, Jordan, Algeria, Zambia, Israel, Italy, and El Salvador. Young people who want to give two years of service through the Quakers rather than the Peace Corps have also been sent to help in local community development efforts in Guatemala, Tanzania, and India.

It is sometimes difficult at first for the local people to understand why the Quakers have come. Are they missionaries? Are they trying to make propaganda for the United States? Are they agents of the capitalists? Generally, however, the Quaker workers have won the trust and respect of the local people. During the 1967 Middle East crisis, when the American embassy in Algiers was threatened by an angry mob, the Quaker team in Skikda was treated with usual courtesy.

When the American Friends Service Committee was first developed, all the major Quaker groups supported it. Meetings throughout the United States raised money, gathered and shipped bales of clothing, and sent seeds and tools to support the Quaker workers overseas. Cooperating in support of their service organization proved a wonderful way of uniting the divided Quaker groups.

It would be a mistake, however, to think that all Quakers are behind the AFSC. To some, the Service Committee efforts to end the Cold War and to increase communication with Russia,

China, and other Communist nations has seemed naive, or even a little disloyal. Other Quakers feel that the Service Committee's work may be humanitarian, but cannot be regarded as religious. What has become of the evangelical fervor of the early Friends, these critics ask? The AFSC, with its roots deep in East Coast Quakerism, never encourages its staff to proselytize, though when asked what Quakers believe, they readily answer. To some pastoral Quakers this does not appear to be nearly enough.

On the other hand, the AFSC has attracted the support of many people of different religious faiths who like the Quakers' practical and direct ways, believe them to be honest, and feel that it is important to support some organization that nourishes the development of new ideas and new ways of solving problems. More than half of the support of the AFSC comes from non-Quakers.

The Vietnam war brought some of these differences of point of view to a head and produced new ones. Some of the more conservative Quakers were pained by the effort of the AFSC to bring medical relief to North, as well as South, Vietnam. Naturally, the former attracted more public attention than the latter, and it therefore developed the wrong public image of Quakerism, these troubled Friends felt.

At the other extreme, the AFSC has seemed entirely too conservative to a small group of Quakers who would like to get back to the old days when Friends were unafraid to challenge the government and to go to jail for their convictions. In particular, these Quakers objected to the fact that in order to ship medical supplies to North Vietnam the AFSC applied for, and obtained, a license from the United States Treasury Office. They believed that the United States Government had no right to demand a license for humanitarian relief, particularly since war had not been declared and therefore North Vietnam could not be considered the enemy. Having formed an organization called A Quaker Action Group, they sent supplies without license, by delivering them across the Canadian border and by taking them directly to Haiphong on board a sloop, the *Phoenix.* Since the United States tried to block these activities, the group was much in the news. The public was naturally confused between these various groups of Friends.

In wartime, the general public hears a lot about the Quakers because of their opposition to military action. In time of peace, the group drops back into obscurity. Nevertheless, since the end of World War I, the Friends have worked diligently for peace in and out of season. They supported the old League of Nations and now support the United Nations. They oppose conscription and counsel young men who seek alternatives to military service. They organize seminars and institutes and publish scholarly studies on international issues. They take part in peace demonstrations and sometimes organize their own. Local Quaker meetings conduct their own peace programs in their local communities and take part in the nationwide efforts of the Friends Committee on National Legislation, the American Friends Service Committee, and the Board on Christian Social Concerns of the Friends United Meeting.

Ever since 1756, when they withdrew from the Pennsylvania Assembly, American Quakers have tended to avoid politics. This is in contrast with the British Quakers, who began to stand for Parliament in the middle of the nineteenth century, and have been quite active since. In the 1950's and 1960's, however, a number of Quakers have stood for public office on a peace platform. Others have become active in various political organizations working for a peace plank in the big national parties.

Modern Quakers do not feel that they have a blueprint for outlawing war in the world. They simply feel, with many other thoughtful people, that this must be done if the human race is to survive. All along they have believed that a man's duty to God is of a higher order than his duty to the state. Now they point out that the Nuremberg trials in which individual Nazis were condemned for following orders rather than their consciences have placed this principle into the body of international law.

Pacifism does not mean nonresistance to evil, Quakers believe. Injustice must be righted and aggression stopped. But the means determine the ends, and violence begets more injustice and aggression. World War I led to World War II, and World War II seems to be leading to World War III. Instead of repeating the weary cycle, modern Quakers believe that we should strengthen world law and look for new and nonviolent ways to confront evil and solve conflicts.

Nonviolent resistance began with the Quakers, was taken up by the New England abolitionists, developed further by Thoreau, influenced by Tolstoy, and finally put into action by Mahatma Gandhi, first in South Africa and then in India. To complete the cycle, present-day Quakers have taken up its study and practice. A Quaker, James Bristol, spent two years in India studying nonviolence and keeping in touch with Gandhi's followers. During this period he was able to arrange a meeting between the latter and the late Martin Luther King, Jr.

Quakers have belonged to several groups in this country which have experimented with the application of nonviolence. These are the Fellowship of Reconciliation and the Committee for Non-Violent Action. CNVA, as it is called, sponsored the sailing of the *Golden Rule* into the forbidden nuclear testing area of the western Pacific in 1958. The organization has also sponsored various demonstrations at nuclear missile sites, and a peace march from Quebec to Guantanamo. Staughton Lynd, a

Quaker who taught at Yale University, wrote the first documentary history of nonviolence in America. Haverford College has an institute for the study of nonviolence.

The most famous use of nonviolence has been that of the late Martin Luther King, Jr., and his Southern Christian Leadership Conference (SCLC) in demonstrating for civil rights. Many Quakers have participated in these demonstrations, in both the North and the South. At Selma, Alabama, an AFSC worker, James Reeb, lost his life. In Chicago, in the summer of 1966, AFSC staff members took part in the Freedom Movement organized by King and led workshops in nonviolence. In Chicago, as earlier in Harlem, Quaker-trained young people helped to avert violence when riots broke out in their neighborhoods. The technique of diverting the direction of a crowd—once used to save the home of Lucretia Mott—was particularly successful. In the summer of 1968 many Quakers went to jail in support of the SCLC Poor People's Campaign.

Some practitioners of nonviolence have spoken of it as a sort of technique, a moral jiujitsu by which the weak can overcome the strong. To the religious Quaker, however, it is an imperative of his Christian faith. If he will accept suffering willingly, as Jesus did, he believes he can introduce a new element into the situation, the power of forgiving love.

William Penn stated this basic belief some three hundred years ago: "A good end cannot sanctify evil means; nor must we ever do evil, that good may come of it. . . . Let us then try what Love will do, for if men did once see we love them, we should soon find they would not harm us."

Modern Quakers often speak of the self-fulfilling prophecy. If you approach a man with fear and hate, you are apt to provoke a hostile response. In colonial times, Quakers refused to believe that the Indian was a fiend bent on violence, and as a result reaped years and years of border peace. In Vietnam, three hundred years later, Quaker workers moved with impunity between areas held by South Vietnam and by Viet Cong troops. "We know the Quakers," a local leader said. "They are the Americans who carry no guns."

The expectation of good rather than evil has helped to protect Quaker workers on the battlefields of the world. Right after World War I a twenty-year-old Quaker boy was assigned the job of taking oxcarts of food over a lonely mountain road from the sea to the city of Pec, in Serbia. He was offered a military guard, but refused. One day he was stopped on a mountain pass and ordered to turn over the supplies. He refused, saying, "These are not mine to give; they are for starving women and children. Will you help me deliver them?" Surprised, the bandit agreed and conducted the young man across the mountain to safety.

In the interests of their concern for peace, modern Quakers have traveled all over the world—to attend conferences on nonviolence, to appeal to the world's leaders for talks rather than acts of war, to give Quakers at home a firsthand report of crisis situations. During the past fifty years, the American Friends have become an exceedingly well-traveled group. Following the example of William Penn, they have made it a point to learn the indigenous tongue wherever they go. In Algeria, Quaker workers learn Arabic and use it rather than the French of the colonial period. In Vietnam, they speak Vietnamese. As much as possible they eat and sleep on the same standard as the people they work among.

During the twentieth century, the Friends United Meeting and the evangelical yearly meetings have continued their missionary efforts in Africa, Jamaica, the Middle East, India, Alaska, Formosa, and Central and South America, making converts as well as building schools and social centers. Partly as a result of these efforts, and those of the British Friends, Quakerism has become a world movement.

There were in 1968 some 42,000 Quakers in Africa (32,000 in Kenya), 1,800 in Asia, 1,600 in Australia and New Zealand, 21,000 in England, 3,000 in Europe, and 6,000 in Latin America.

The little pockets of Quakerism need the stimulation of frequent meetings. To a certain extent this is supplied by visiting Friends. Quakers still have a strong sense of mission to visit Friends meetings in other lands. They also like to travel, and there is in consequence a steady stream of visitors at most Quaker outposts.

Since 1937, the work of keeping in touch with Friends far and near has been augmented by the formation of a group called the Friends World Committee for Consultation. From offices in England and the United States, this organization encourages intervisitation and develops meetings on subjects of special interest to Quakers. It also sponsors world conferences, attended by representatives of all Quaker groups on the face of the globe.

In August of 1967, the fourth such conference was held on the grounds of Guilford College, North Carolina, with some nine hundred Friends representing thirty-one nations in attendance. In preparation for the conference, two study books were prepared, and Friends in their meetinghouses throughout the world discussed the topics of the books for months before the conference took place. The conference was planned not to reach conclusions or to plan a precise course of action, but simply to help Friends from around the world come a little closer to understanding each other.

At the conference itself there were hopeful signs that such understanding was beginning to develop. Sitting together in small study groups, the evangelical Friends learned that the liberal eastern Friends were not as irreligious as they feared, while the easterners detected signs of change and ferment in their more conservative fellow members. It was recognized that each of the three groups had chosen to emphasize different aspects of early Quakerdom—the evangelical outreach, the pastoral caring for one another, the tradition of silent worship.

The theme of the Guilford Conference was taken from a letter by George Fox to his parents: "We have no Time but this Present Time, therefore prize your time for your soul's sake." Friends, hurtled from the quiet of their nineteenth-century seclusion into the thick of world affairs by their testimony for peace, hope that in the world of today theirs is an idea whose present time has come.

Quakers rally for peace outside of Independence Hall in Philadelphia. (*Photo by Ted Hetzel.*)

# 10

# American Quakers today

Recently a freshman at the University of Pennsylvania complained to his dancing partner, "Six months in Philadelphia and I haven't seen a single Quaker!"

"Well, cheer up, you're dancing with one now," the girl replied.

Quakers have long since discarded the Quaker gray, the broad-brimmed hat, and the Quaker bonnet, which were once their distinguishing marks. Other Quaker ways have disappeared, too. If modern Friends use "thee" it is only within their immediate family. The prohibition against art, music, and theater is regarded as the sad mistake of another age. Quakers, a predominantly middle-class group, share the tastes and interests of most middle-class Americans.

And yet one Quaker can usually recognize another in a crowd. There is a penchant for a simple, direct style of dress, a habit of understatement, and a directness of approach which most Quakers share. In addition the birthright Friends, the descendants of the old Quaker families, bear a certain resemblance resulting from common ancestors. There is a Quaker look, just as there is a Yankee look, although it is difficult to describe.

Since the Quakers have remained a small group in society, the old Quaker families are generally interrelated. From Maine to California genealogy quickly becomes a topic of conversation whenever birthright Quakers meet. The years of isolation, of persecution, and of the championing of lost causes have developed among Quakers a family feeling rather unusual in the modern world. One Quaker is welcome in the home of another at almost any time and place. This fellowship is not reserved for the "old" Quakers, but extended to the convinced as well.

Quaker family life itself has contributed over the years to the development of a tribal feeling. In earlier generations, fathers and mothers conscientiously prepared their children to become useful members of the Society of Friends. Discipline was gentle, but anger and quarreling were discouraged, and thoughtfulness and unselfishness valued over self-expression. Quakers were taught to conform to their family and their Society, though they were nonconformists to the outside world.

Quakers have always believed that the best way to resolve a conflict is to bring it out into the open and find a creative solution. Like other people, however, they sometimes short cut this process by simply pretending that the conflict doesn't exist. In the day to day practice of family life there was undoubtedly a good bit of the latter in Quaker families. Some Quaker psychologists have noted a tendency among Friends to refuse to face their own anger, or to turn it inward.

Modern Quaker parents tend to take their role just as seriously as their predecessors, but their goal is sometimes different. They often have studied child care, and they endeavor to raise their children in the best interests of mental health. Many have reacted against their own childhood training and have given their youngsters more scope for the open expression of feeling than they were given. Whether or not this change will result in any discernible difference in another generation of Quakers is difficult to judge.

One thing can be said for a Quaker upbringing: it fits men and women to adapt themselves easily, even happily, into group behavior. Quakers today have committees to deal with everything. The Friends Committee on National Legislation represents Friends' interests in Washington. The American Friends Service Committee expresses Quaker concerns. The Friends Council on Education is a clearinghouse for Friends schools. The Friends World Committee keeps Quakers around the globe in contact with each other and nurses along new meetings. Three large confederations serve the various varieties of Friends: Friends General Conference—the liberal, silent meetings; Friends United Meeting—the more conservative groups both programed and unprogramed; Friends Evangelical Alliance—the Evangelical Quakers. All three have staff, conferences, and various activities. Yearly, quarterly, and monthly meetings have many projects of their own.

Quakers serve on the subcommittees of these organizations and scores like them, on the boards of schools and colleges, on meeting committees in abundance. The surprising thing to many people is that Quakers actually enjoy going to a lot of meetings.

There is a great deal of laughter and warmth in a Quaker committee meeting, and though the individual Quaker may occasionally grumble about the number he attends, he will usually also admit that they are a lot of fun.

In order to free themselves to devote time and energy to their committees and their pursuit of Quaker concerns, Friends today continue to practice Quaker simplicity. This is expressed today not by the adherence to certain rules—wearing Quaker gray, avoiding fiction—but by a certain style of life. Quakers try hard not to keep up with the Joneses. To move one's family halfway across the country in search of a slightly higher salary, a slightly better status, a slightly bigger car is to be trapped by the unimportant material aspects of life. By keeping their standard of living simple, Quakers feel, they can keep themselves free—free from making compromises, free to speak their minds—free to entertain often and easily, free to drop everything and go overseas for several years on a service assignment, free to devote themselves to spiritual rather than material growth.

This simplicity is a relative thing. There are some rather wealthy Quaker families who live quietly but comfortably, and use their wealth to support Quaker institutions. And there are many young Quaker couples who scrape along on the salary of a public school teacher or a beginning social worker in order to continue to do the thing they believe in. In recent years the tendency has been more and more in the direction of education and social work, and the number of prosperous Quaker businessmen has become correspondingly less. Some older Quakers deplore this, feeling there will not be enough wealth accumulated to keep the Quaker schools and colleges operating under Quaker auspices. To younger and more radical Quakers, however, it is a sign that the Society is coming out of the doldrums back into a period of intense commitment.

During the past twenty-five years the actual number of Quakers in America has gained only 18 per cent, while the population as a whole has grown at more than twice this rate; in other words, the Quakers are losing ground. With only 120,000 members in a population of 200 million, they are a small remnant indeed. There is a steady attrition by death of the many elderly members, and the drifting away of young birthright members with no real interest in the Society of Friends. On the other hand there is a small but steady trickle of new members by convincement—men and women from a wide variety of backgrounds who find in Quakerism the only kind of religion they feel to be meaningful to them. Particularly the new unprogramed meetings on college campuses, those in the city, and those in exurbanite communities are made up primarily of these Quakers by convincement.

This process is quite remarkable because Friends of the silent meeting variety make absolutely no effort to recruit new members. Although their spiritual ancestors were evangelical, colonial Friends by 1740 were taking a rather standoffish attitude toward conversion and religious enthusiasm. This mood, understandably annoying to the more evangelical Friends, has persisted on the East Coast to this day. Many members of silent meetings have confessed it took months of quiet persistence to attend meeting in the face of an attitude of reserve on the part of the older members.

When they finally crash this barrier and join the Society, convinced Friends often bring with them some of the enthusiasm and fire of early Quakerdom. Having found the Quaker way after a long religious search they feel they have discovered the availability of religious experience "experientially" just as Fox and his followers did long ago. They are often stronger adherents of the peace testimony and the race testimony than birthright Quakers. To become a Quaker today means embracing some unpopular beliefs. It is not an easy decision to make. Those who have made it are often more ready to stand up and be counted than those who were born into the Society.

With their fire and drive, the convinced Friends also bring with them—sometimes unconsciously—the religious images and language of their background, whether it is Catholic, Episcopalian, Methodist, or Jewish. Since Quakerism has no set creed, and since the unprogramed meeting is formless, it is easy for these newcomers to read into the Society those things they would like to hear and see. Like the tale about the three blind men, each holding on to a different limb of an elephant and describing what he felt, each new Friend grabs onto Quakerism and describes it as he experiences it. This can be enriching to a meeting, but it can also make Quakerism so diffuse that the inner core of its meaning is threatened.

Quakers worry about the diffuseness. Among the unprogramed meetings there is a growing trend to schedule courses in Quaker history for the newer members, or to organize discussion groups on the meaning of Quakerism. Among programed meetings, a similar search for identity has led to the development of a School of Religion at Earlham College, where Quaker pastors can be trained, as well as leaders for unprogramed meetings. Previously the programed meetings had drawn pastors from schools of religion sponsored by other denominations. The result was a dilution of Quakerism as confusing as that experienced by some of the unprogramed meetings.

In recent years the silent Quaker meetings have attracted a number of men and women of Jewish background who have rejected the theology of their past and are often attracted to Quakerism on humanitarian grounds. According to an old joke, a prominent New York rabbi is supposed to have complained, "Some of my best Jews are Friends."

In 1967, one such man of Jewish background joined the

Society of Friends, having stated on his application, "I am a Jewish Friend, I am not a Christian." He was, he said, in unity with Friends on many matters, but he thought of the religious growth he was experiencing among Friends as a continuation rather than a repudiation of his Jewish background. "The language of religious experience and ethical teaching I am most at home with comes from the historical milieu of Judaism," he stated. "The language of Christianity is largely opaque to me."

This event produced a flurry of letters in the *Friends Journal,* the principal publication read by Eastern Friends. Some hailed the acceptance of the man's application as a formal acknowledgment of a process that had been going on for some time. Others regretted the action of the meeting in accepting the application. Early Quakerism, these letter writers said, had been an effort to return to basic primitive Christianity. If modern Quakerism lost this central core of meaning it would make the Society little more than a philosophical grouping of humanists. If the "Jewish Friend" had not been ready to accept Quaker history as it was, why had he not joined the Wider Quaker Fellowship? This group was created to solve this very problem and to accommodate Hindus, Jews, Moslems, and others who, while holding on to their own religion, wanted to express their unity with Friends.

Behind the controversy lurks a larger question that bubbles and boils within the Society of Friends. Most Quakers agree that Quakerism is a Christian movement, and that it will serve society best by preserving its identity. The issue is: shall this identity be preserved by asking all members to agree on any statement of belief? Some Friends seem to be asking for a pledge of Christian faith. Others, remembering the tragedy of separation, prefer to avoid creeds, just as their ancestors did, and to trust the individual to find for himself, experientially, the same truth which their ancestors experienced in silence. The terms in which he describes this experience, according to this argument, is a matter of semantics. It is the vitality of the experience that counts.

Today the walls which Quakers used to protect themselves from the world are all but gone. The hope of the Society for any sort of continued existence seems to rest on a renewal of the vitality which created it in the first place. This vitality came from the ability of the Society of Friends to answer the needs of the seventeenth century; it can only be recaptured if this small religious body finds out how to meet the needs of today.

Here and there are signs that this is happening. A few monthly meetings show signs of renewing themselves, as young people join, not out of a conventional need for some sort of religious affiliation but an honest search for inner experience, for integrity, for brotherhood—the same search that sends other young people into experimentation with drugs. Symbolically, one group of young Quakers has rented the former office of a psychedelic center.

Philadelphia Yearly Meeting, traditionally one of the most conservative of Quaker bodies, was shaken to its roots in the spring of 1967 when a group of young Quakers urged that it support the ship *Phoenix* in delivering drugs to North Vietnam without United States State Department approval. Many middle-aged Friends were originally opposed, but yielded to the spirit of the meeting when older Quakers rose one after the other to urge support of the youth. Gradually a feeling of unity developed within the meeting as though a giant bell had been struck, and was ringing true. Historically minded Friends wondered if it had been like that on the day that John Woolman persuaded the Quakers, against their self-interest, to begin to release their slaves.

No matter how permissive it becomes about accepting new members, the Society of Friends will probably never become a mass religion. Only a minority of Americans will enjoy the austerity of its worship, or want to involve themselves in a way of life that demands a total commitment. But through the years that lie ahead, the Society of Friends will support individuals who believe that the world can be made better, and who want to experiment with new ways to make it so. America would be poorer without this wellspring of new ideas.

Chagrin Falls Park Work Camp (*Photo by Beth Binford*)

# Epilogue

This book was originally written in 1967-68, when U.S. protest against the war in Vietnam was accelerating, and when American Quakers found themselves called upon to give support and leadership to a burgeoning anti-war movement which shared their political position but not necessarily their religious motivation or commitment to nonviolence. Should Friends give their name to protest marches in which some groups planned to provoke the police or the National Guard? Should they sponsor films which not only protested the American presence in Vietnam but seemed wholly uncritical of the Vietnamese communists? Should they provide sanctuary in their meetinghouses for those who left military duty without leave because of conscientious objection to the war? Or help young men who were fleeing to Canada to avoid the draft?

These were the sorts of dilemmas which preoccupied meetings and individual Friends during the late 1960s.

This period of vigorous challenge and searching resulted in a commitment to a more activist form of nonviolence. As members of the Vietnam generation came to work for Quaker organizations such as the American Friends Service Committee and the Friends Committee on National Legislation, or to teach in Quaker schools, they helped remind Friends of their early radical roots.

Other changes taking place in American society began to have an impact on the Society of Friends in the late 1960s and early 1970s. The Black Power movement, emerging out of the civil rights movement of the early 1960s (which Friends had fully supported) created new pressures for change. In 1970, a group of Black Friends and their friends sat in at Philadelphia Yearly Meeting and demanded reparations for past injustice. The response was the establishment of a special fund for the economic development of Black enterprises, set up by the Yearly Meeting at its session in March 1971. At about the same time, a group of Black and other Third World staff members of the AFSC established a Third World Coalition to provide mutual support for Third World staff and to strengthen their impact on the hiring as well as program decisions of the Committee. Quaker schools and colleges, feeling similar pressures, began to work to improve minority enrollment, as well to strive for a more diverse faculty. Exchanges between inner city and suburban Quaker schools were promoted. The Friends United Meeting, representing midwestern "pastoral" Friends, established its first inner city mission, in Chicago.

The youth rebellion on the campuses was peaking in the spring of 1968 with the student explosion at Columbia University in New York. This development, too, had a strong effect on American Quakers. Within AFSC a group of young people, who called themselves "Flowers Under Thirty," began to press for programs in which young people had decision-making status, rather than programs designed to enhance their social education. This led to a gradual decline in the number of workcamps and other programs designed to attract middle-class youth, and to a a series of structural changes within AFSC. As a result, more projects today are planned to involve Third World youth in their own communities. For example, in San Francisco, young people in predominantly Black areas counsel their peers on alternatives to entering the military. Quaker schools and colleges during the period moved rapidly toward involving students in decisions about campus life and discipline. At Pendle Hill and at larger Quaker gatherings, sessions were offered to help Friends understand the rapidly changing lifestyles of the new generation. Helping more conservative Friends accept these changes, Quaker historians such as Henry J. Cadbury reminded members of the Society that the first generation of Friends had been young rebels too.

Along with the Black Power movement and the youth movement came the reemergence of the women's movement and its new demands for the elimination of sexist language and stereotyped roles in the family and the office. Having always considered themselves pioneers in women's rights, many Friends at first thought that the new movement had little relevance to the Society, in which women had always played strong roles. However, the demand for the correction of sexist language brought a surprisingly negative response in many meetings, and some older men and women were not initially very comfortable with the challenge to sex roles, such as female responsibility for the covered dish supper and male responsibility for the meeting's property. Gradually it became clear that the ways of the world had infiltrated the Society of Friends, allowing subtle sexism to develop and creating strong, if unconscious, resistance to the development of a feminist consciousness.

An interest in exploring the relationship between feminism and

Quakerism, both historically and in the present, sprang to life as a result, and spread throughout the Society. Many women in the Evangelical Friends Alliance became interested in exploring their feminist roots, and developed a correspondence network. A woman from an evangelical background, Kara Cole, was selected as the head of Friends United Meeting, headquartered in Richmond, Indiana. Many young women entered training for the ministry at the Earlham School of Religion, recalling the role of the early Quaker women ministers. Among the silent-meeting Friends, a network of women developed around the Friends General Conference gatherings. In 1974, a newsletter, *Friendly Woman*, was begun, and in 1976 women presented a dramatization of the 1876 Centennial celebration in Philadelphia, where Susan B. Anthony and her friends interrupted the proceedings to proclaim women's rights. There have been annual women's meetings since, and a second newsletter, *The Friendly Nuisance*, has linked attenders.

Many strong women have played a role in the American Friends Service Committee from its birth in 1927, but in 1980 Asia Bennett became the first woman Executive Secretary of the organization. A nationwide Women's Program, developed by a women's coalition, keeps an eye on affirmative action and the development of programs with a feminist component.

The response to Black Power, the youth rebellion, and the women's movement has been largely internal to the Society, stimulating changes in Quaker perspectives and institutions. Meanwhile Friends have continued to be deeply concerned about, and involved in, world problems. AFSC was active on both sides of the Nigeria/Biafra war, and was able to play a role in conciliation, recorded in a book, *Quaker Experiences in International Conciliation* by C. H. Yarrow (Yale University Press). Anguished by the U.S. bombing and invasion of Cambodia, American Friends were among the first to enter that country after the defeat of Pol Pot, and to bring the suffering of the Cambodian people to the attention of the world. A major focus of recent Quaker outreach has been the growing desertification and resulting famine in the Sahel region of Africa.

Friends in both the United States and Great Britain have long been opposed to apartheid in South Africa. Early efforts to intervene constructively have included the support of a Quaker social worker in Soweto to work with the families of Black detainees, and the establishment of an exchange program between the U.S. and South Africa to increase dialogue on racial problems. As, year after year, apartheid has continued, Friends have felt the need to rid themselves of all complicity in the system, and have therefore questioned the acceptability of travelling in South Africa, and of investing money there. A vigorous debate has taken place in several Yearly Meetings and Quaker Colleges over the appropriateness of withdrawing all investments or mounting an economic boycott as a nonviolent tool to press South Africa toward change. Some Friends feel that a boycott will only stiffen the backs of the advocates of apartheid and will cause Black workers themselves to suffer. Black African leaders generally dismiss this danger. AFSC, at work both in Zambia, since its independence in 1964, and more recently in Zimbabwe, has come to know many of the Black leaders of the anti-apartheid movement and has been responsive to their pleas for economic disengagement.

The growing U.S. involvement in Central America has been a cause of concern to American Quakers for some time. Many Friends have seen an ominous similarity between the military buildup in that region, and the efforts to support rebels in destabilizing the government of Nicaragua, and the beginning of U.S. intervention in Vietnam. Some Friends have gone to Honduras to visit the Salvadoran refugee camps, hoping to provide by their presence some security against paramilitary raids across the border, while helping to meet refugee health and occupation needs. Others have joined a nonviolent witness for peace along the Nicaraguan border. Within the United States, some meetings have expressed their concern by declaring sanctuary for Central American refugees, openly housing Salvadorans who are in this country illegally because the United States government has refused to consider their pleas for political asylum. Other Friends have helped some of these refugees slip through the country into Canada, or live in concealment here, in a manner reminiscent of the underground railroad of pre-Civil War days.

Not all Friends share these activities or concerns. The Evangelical Friends have been establishing new Friends churches in Central America, particularly in Guatemala, which address spiritual concerns exclusively. These Friends see the activities of the "liberal" Quakers as too political, and sometimes as too left-wing. The three large bodies of American Friends continue to differ considerably on the relationship of the spiritual life to social action, with the eastern group the most liberal, the western the most conservative, and the midwestern in between. Since there were both political and evangelical sides to the early Quaker movement in George Fox's time, both claim the vindication of historical precedent.

Other concerns divide the three groups. The Biblical orientation of the more conservative Friends makes them less accepting of the concept of supporting civil rights for gay men and lesbians, a position taken by some of the eastern Yearly Meetings in recent years and incorporated into the affirmative action programs of the American Friends Service Committee. There is also disagreement over the issue of abortion.

Two issues, however, have served in the past decade and a half to bring Friends closer. One is the concern for equal rights for women, as previously mentioned. The other is the continuing concern for peace. The pastoral and evangelical Friends have remained faithful to the peace testimony, producing more conscientious objectors than the liberal eastern meetings. With the heightened threat of nuclear war, they have been increasingly concerned to find a way for Friends as a group to make a difference.

In 1970, the Evangelical Friends Alliance invited all Yearly Meetings of groups calling themselves members of the Religious Society of Friends to a national conference in St. Louis to explore common threads of faith and practice. Out of this conference emerged the faith and life movement, which produced some pamphlets designed to reacquaint Friends with their common heritage, and which issued "A New Call to Peacemaking," addressed to all Friends as well as to Mennonites and Brethren. The object of this call was to explore new ways for the peace churches to express the historic peace testimony. Significantly, the most common outcome of the New Call to Peacemaking has been a growing interest in tax refusal as a nonviolent method of protesting war.

Since the earliest times, Friends have refused to pay war taxes, but they have been less clear about paying taxes "in the mixture," that is, taxes which go for both war and peaceful purposes. Since the end of the Second World War, some Friends have been refusing to pay that portion of their income tax which goes to support past, present, and future wars, and a few have kept their income below the taxable level in order to avoid the whole problem of liability. It has, however, been an issue on which Friends could not agree, some saying that the graduated income tax is the fairest way to spread the tax burden and provide services for the poor in a democracy, and others pointing out that to refuse to pay fifty percent of one's tax only means that the government could take "war taxes" out of the remaining fifty percent. Ultimately, such critics point out, the IRS collects anyway, through fines or levies, and to pretend otherwise is not honest. Debates on the subject have been held in Friends gatherings and in the pages of Friends publications.

In recent years, the drift toward nuclear war has made more converts to tax refusal, and more and more monthly and yearly meetings are passing minutes expressing their willingness to support those of their members who take such a stand, and to wrestle with their own consciences. Other peace churches are reviewing the issue. It is hoped that if all got together in a common stand against war taxes, it would ultimately have the same impact as the common stand against compulsory military service in World Wars I and II.

Friends' concerns, it should be reiterated, always begin with an individual who feels he or she has a strong leading, and who follows conscience without calculating the political results. The heart of the matter is the individual's need to stay in touch with the Divine Spirit. But if the leading is a true one, it is transmitted sooner or later through the Quaker group process into a group concern and group action. A broad-based nonviolent campaign against supporting war through the payment of taxes has seemed to many Quaker historians to be the next logical step in the evolution of the Quaker testimony against war.

Closely related to the concern for peace has always been the concern to live simply. John Woolman, the Quaker abolitionist, once urged Friends to look to their possessions to see if they contained the seeds of war. In the vocabulary of today, Friends are careful not to use a disproportionate share of the world's resources. The ecology movement of the 1970s, with its emphasis on the shrinking availability of those resources on planet earth, deepened the interest among Friends in living as simply and as much in harmony with the natural world as possible. Some sought a simpler lifestyle for themselves and their families in rural areas in Maine, Vermont, West Virginia, Northern California, Oregon, and other areas. Others joined simple living collectives in the city. One of these, a group in San Francisco, published a best-selling book, *Taking Charge*, recently republished as *Taking Charge of Our Lives* (Harper & Row).

Jolted by the changes of the 1960s and 1970s, the Society of Friends in the United States today appears to be moving from a long period of relative stability and adjustment to the society at large into a phase in which its historic role as prophet and critic demands more of it and its members. Periods of quietness and activism have always alternated. Friends appear now to be preparing for a period of activism. This change seems reflected in membership. While some of the older centers of Quakerism are showing stable or even declining memberships, the newer small, silent Yearly Meetings in the midwest and on the west coast appear to be growing, as members of the Vietnam generation, enjoying delayed parenthood, are seeking a religious base for themselves and their children.

Worldwide, the rapid growth of Friends churches in Africa and Latin America has led to a prediction that by 1990 more than half of the members of the Society of Friends will be from the Third World. While some of these newer converts to an evangelical form of Quakerism might find the liberal Friends somewhat strange, the concerns for equality and peace continue to characterize Friends everywhere. As the long-time White Anglo-Saxon hold on the Society diminishes, Quaker institutions and organizations feel the pressure to make their boards, committees and staff more inclusive. This too leads to change.

Young Friends becoming active in the Society today thus are faced with the historic opportunity to provide new ideas and new leadership for the next surge ahead. The growing worldwide anti-war movement, with its interest in nonviolence, in feminism and in simplicity, heightens receptivity to the Quaker message. This is no time for quietism and despair. Rather it is a time of renewal for the ebullient, positive, evangelical spirit of the first generation of quiet rebels.

Quang Ngai Rehabilitation Center (*Courtesy the American Friends Service Committee.*)

# ✁ Bibliography

## HISTORY, GENERAL

*Friends for 300 Years.* Howard Brinton. New York: Harpers, 1952.

*The Quakers in Peace and War.* M. E. Hirst. London: Swarthmore Press Limited, 1923.

*The Discovery of Quakerism.* Harold Loukes. London: George G. Harrap & Co., 1960.

*The Quaker Contribution.* Harold Loukes. New York: Macmillan, 1965.

*The History of Quakerism.* Elbert Russell. New York: Macmillan, 1942.

*The Quakers: A New Look at Their Place in Society.* John Sykes. Philadelphia: J. B. Lippincott Co., 1959.

*A History of the Friends in America.* Allen and Richard Thomas. Philadelphia: John C. Winston Co., 1905.

*The People Called Quakers.* D. Elton Trueblood. New York: Harpers, 1966.

*The Story of Quakerism.* Elfrida Vipont. London: The Bannisdale Press, 1954.

*Quaker Reflections to Light the Future.* Foreword by Henry Cadbury. Philadelphia: Friends General Conference, 1967.

## HISTORY, SPECIAL SUBJECTS

*Quaker Education in Theory and Practice.* Howard H. Brinton. Wallingford, Pa.: Pendle Hill Pamphlet No. 9, 1940.

*William Penn's "Holy Experiment."* Edwin B. Bronner. Philadelphia: Temple University Publications, 1962.

*Quakers and Slavery in America.* Thomas E. Drake. New Haven, Connecticut: Yale University Press, 1950.

*American Friends in World Missions.* Christina H. Jones. Elgin, Illinois: Brethren Publishing House, 1946.

*Quakers in the American Colonies.* Rufus M. Jones. London: Macmillan, 1923.

*Later Periods of Quakerism, Vols. I and II.* Rufus M. Jones. London: Macmillan, 1921.

*The Quakers as Pioneers in Social Work.* Auguste Jorns. New York: Macmillan, 1931.

*Friends and the Indians.* Rayner Wickersham Kelsey. Philadelphia: The Associated Executive Committee of Friends on Indian Affairs, 1917.

*Meeting House and Counting House.* Frederick B. Tolles. Chapel Hill, North Carolina: University of North Carolina Press, 1948.

*Quaker Adventures.* Edward Thomas. New York: Fleming H. Revell Co., 1928.

*Quakers and the Atlantic Culture.* Frederick B. Tolles. New York: Macmillan, 1960.

*Friends in New York.* William H. S. Wood. New York: Privately printed, 1904.

*Friends Asylum for the Insane 1813–1913.* Philadelphia: John C. Winston Co., 1913.


## BIOGRAPHY AND AUTOBIOGRAPHY

*Jane Addams, A Centennial Reader.* Margaret Tis. New York: Macmillan, 1961.

*Moses Brown, Reluctant Reformer.* Mack Thompson, Chapel Hill: University of North Carolina Press, 1962.

*Cornelia, the Story of a Civil War Nurse.* Jane McConnell. New York: Thomas Y. Crowell, 1959.

*Prudence Crandall: Woman of Courage.* Elizabeth Yates. New York: Alladin Books, 1955.

*Bear His Mild Yoke—The Story of Mary Dyer.* Ethel White. New York: Abingdon Press, 1966.

*Life of Thomas Eddy.* London: Samuel Knapp, 1836.

*Journal of George Fox.* Edited by John L. Nickalls. Cambridge, England: University Press, 1952.

*George Fox and the Quakers.* Henry Van Etten. New York: Harper & Row (Harper Torchbooks), 1959.

*Elias Hicks, Quaker Liberal.* Bliss Forbush. New York: Columbia University Press, 1956.

*Isaac T. Hopper.* L. Maria Child. Boston: John P. Jewett & Company, 1853.

*Friend of Life. The Biography of Rufus Jones.* Elizabeth Gray Vining. Philadelphia: J. B. Lippincott Company, 1958.

*James Logan and the Culture of Provincial America.* Frederick B. Tolles. Boston: Little, Brown and Co., 1957.

*Lucretia Mott.* Otelia Cromwell. Cambridge: Harvard University Press, 1958.

*William Penn. A Biography.* Catherine Owens Peare. Philadelphia: J. B. Lippincott Company, 1957.

*For More Than Bread.* Clarence Pickett. Boston: Little, Brown and Co., 1953.

*John Greenleaf Whittier.* John Pollard. Boston: Houghton Mifflin, 1949.

*John Woolman, American Quaker.* Janet Whitney. Boston: Little, Brown and Co., 1942.

*Journal of John Woolman* (John G. Whittier edition). Introduction by Frederick B. Tolles. New York: Corinth Books, 1961.

## QUAKERISM, GENERAL

*Creative Worship.* Howard Brinton. Wallingford, Pa.: Pendle Hill
Publications, 1957.

*American Quakers Today.* Edwin Bronner. Philadelphia: Friends
World Committee, 1966.

*The Quaker Approach.* Edited by Jack Kavanaugh. New York:
G. P. Putnam Sons, 1953.

*Democracy and the Quaker Method.* Pollard, Pollard and Pollard.
London: Bannisdale Press, 1949.

## RELATED SUBJECTS

*Roads to Agreement.* Stuart Chase. New York: Harper & Row,
1951.

*The Mentally Ill in America.* Albert Deutsch. New York: Columbia
University Press, 1949.

*Nonviolence in America.* Staughton Lynd. Indianapolis: Bobbs-
Merrill Co., 1966.

*They Were in Prison.* Negley K. Teeters. Philadelphia: John C.
Winston Co., 1937.

# Index

# More Resources From
# New Society Publishers

To Order: send check or money order to New Society Publishers, 4722 Baltimore Avenue, Philadelphia, PA 19143. For postage and handling: add $1.50 for the first book and 40 cents for each additional book.

**GANDHI THROUGH WESTERN EYES**
by Horace Alexander

"This book stands out as an authoritative guide: clear, simple, and straightforward, both to Gandhi's personality and to his beliefs. As a Quaker, Mr. Alexander found it easy to grasp Gandhi's ideas about nonviolence; the author's prolonged and intimate friendship helped him to know the Mahatma as few men were able to do, and to appreciate that he was something far greater than a national hero of the Indian independence movement—a man, in fact, with a message that is intensely relevant for the world today. Nothing that has so far been published about Gandhi is more illuminating than this careful, perceptive and comprehensive work. It is not only comprehensive—it is convincing."

—Times Literary Supplement

Letter, Index. 240 pages. 1984.
Hardcover: $24.95
Paperback: $8.95

"This is the bravest book I have read since Jonathan Schell's FATE OF THE EARTH."

—Dr. Rollo May

DESPAIR AND PERSONAL POWER IN THE NUCLEAR AGE
by Joanna Rogers Macy

*Despair and Personal Power in the Nuclear Age* is the first major book to examine our psychological responses to planetary perils and to lay the theoretical foundations for an empowering, personally-centered approach to social change. Included are sections on awakening in the nuclear age, relating to children and young people, guided meditations, empowered rituals, and a special section on "Spiritual Exercises for a Time of Apocalypse." This book was described and excerpted in *New Age Journal* and *Fellowship Magazine*, recommended for public libraries by *Library Journal*, and selected for inclusion in the 1984 Women's Reading Program, General Board of Global Ministries, United Methodist Church.

200 pages. Appendices, resource lists, exercises. 1983.
Hardcover: $19.95
Paperback: $8.95

**REWEAVING THE WEB OF LIFE: FEMINISM AND NONVIOLENCE**
edited by Pam McAllister

"...happens to be one of the most important books you'll ever read."
—*The Village Voice*

"Stressing the connection between patriarchy and war, sex and violence, this book shows that nonviolence can be an assertive, positive force. It's provocative reading for anyone interested in surviving and changing the nuclear age."
—*Ms. Magazine*

More than 50 contributors. Topics include: Women's History, Women and the Struggle Against Militarism, Violence and its Origins, Nonviolence and Women's Self-Defense. A richly varied collection of interviews, songs, poems, stories, provocative proposals, photographs.

Most often recommended book in the 1983 WIN MAGAZINE ANNUAL BOOK POLL

Annotated Bibliography. Index.
448 pages.
Hardcover: $19.95
Paperback: $10.95

**WE ARE ALL PART OF ONE ANOTHER: A BARBARA DEMING READER**
edited with an introduction by Jane Meyerding
Foreword by Barbara Smith

Essays, speeches, letters, stories, poems by America's foremost writer on issues of women and peace, feminism and nonviolence, spanning four decades.

"Barbara Deming always challenges us to rise above easy answers about who we are. Her insight into the nature of political change and the needs of the human spirit makes hers a unique feminist voice which guides and inspires us in the struggle for a more humane world."

—Charlotte Bunch

"Her work continues to be life-sustaining, as necessary as breath to me. This new collection is indeed a treasure."

—Pam McAllister

320 pages. 1984.
Hardcover: $24.95
Paperback: $10.95